Creepy Kawaii

I0490196

A NOTE ABOUT GEL PENS, MARKERS ETC:

All coloring pages are one sided with black on the opposite side to help avoid bleed through. Depending on your media of choice, inks could leak through the paper and onto the next design.

There are some test sheets in the back of the book that you can use to test your markers, pens, etc.

Sign your name, color in a box, draw a doodle. If you find any bleed through, you may want to use a blank sheet of paper between designs.

Thanks!

Gibbous Moon

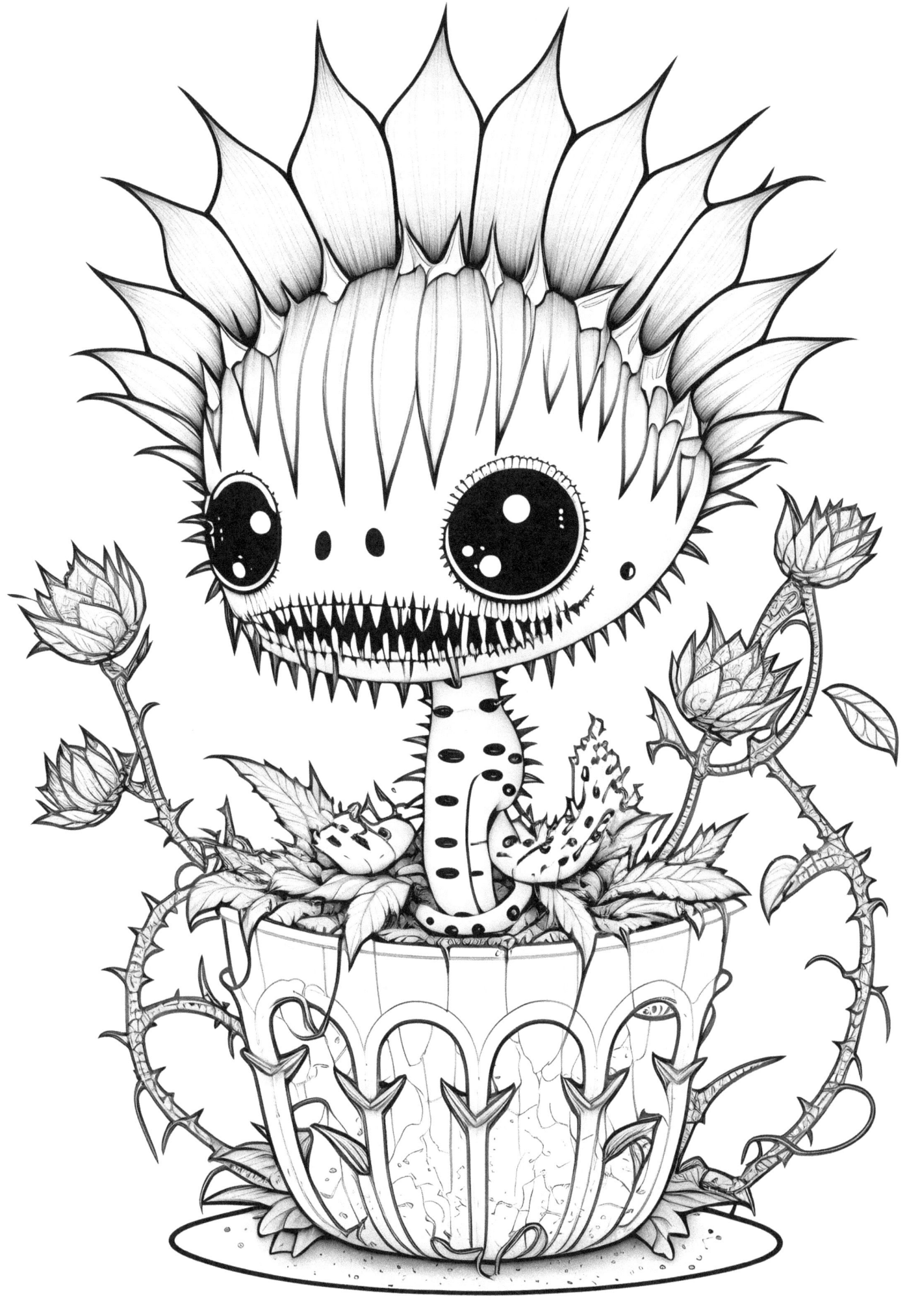

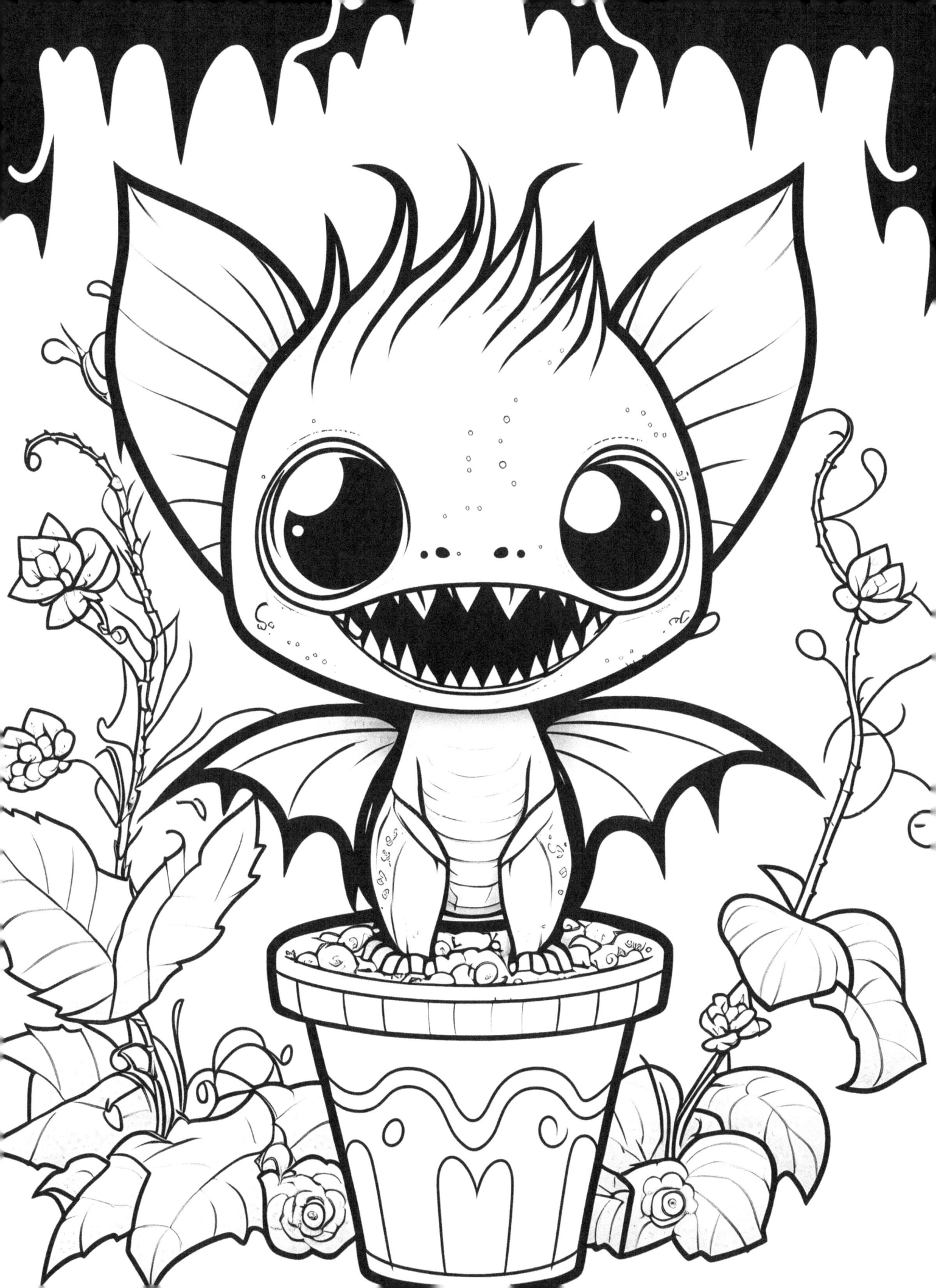

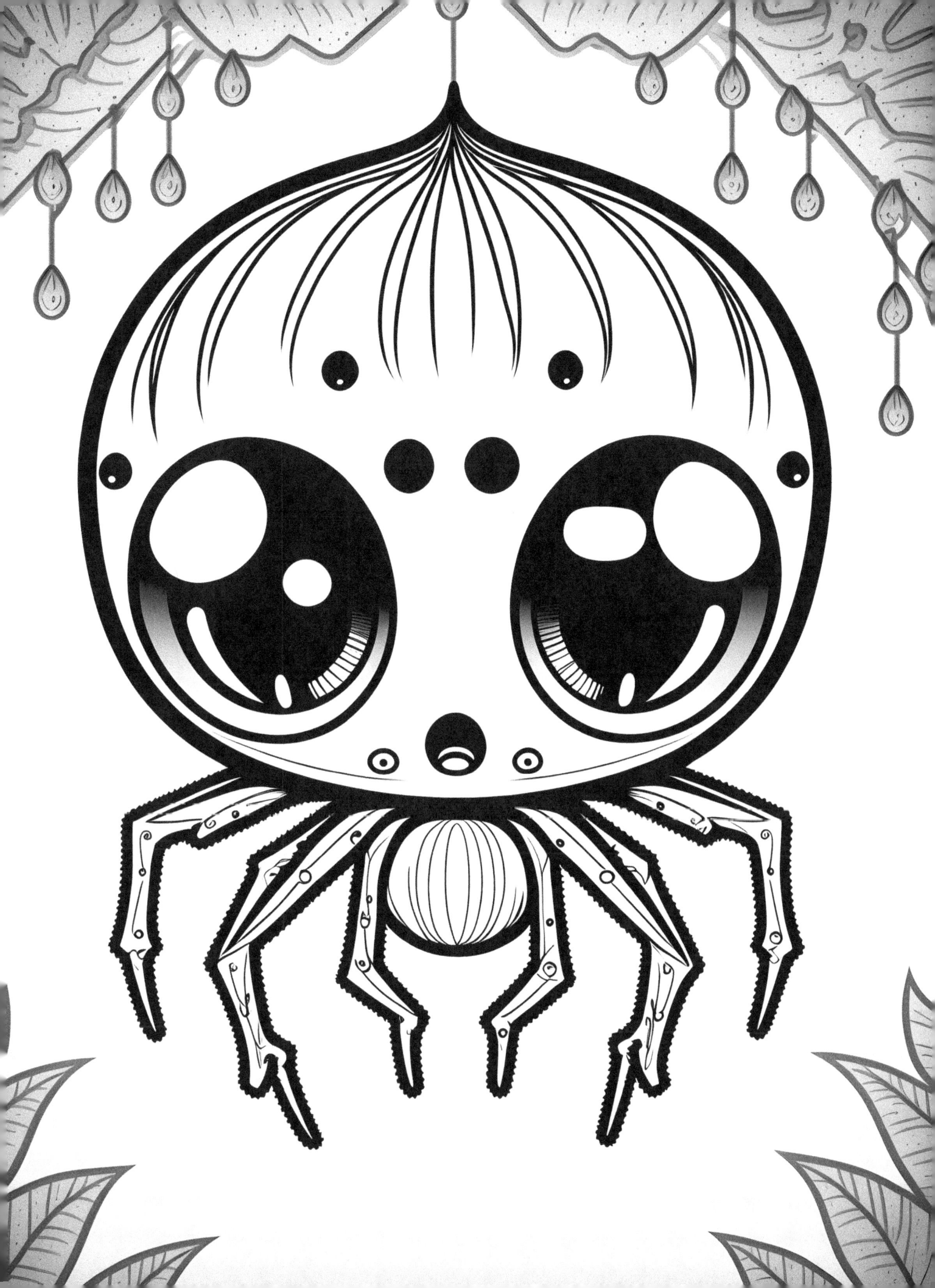

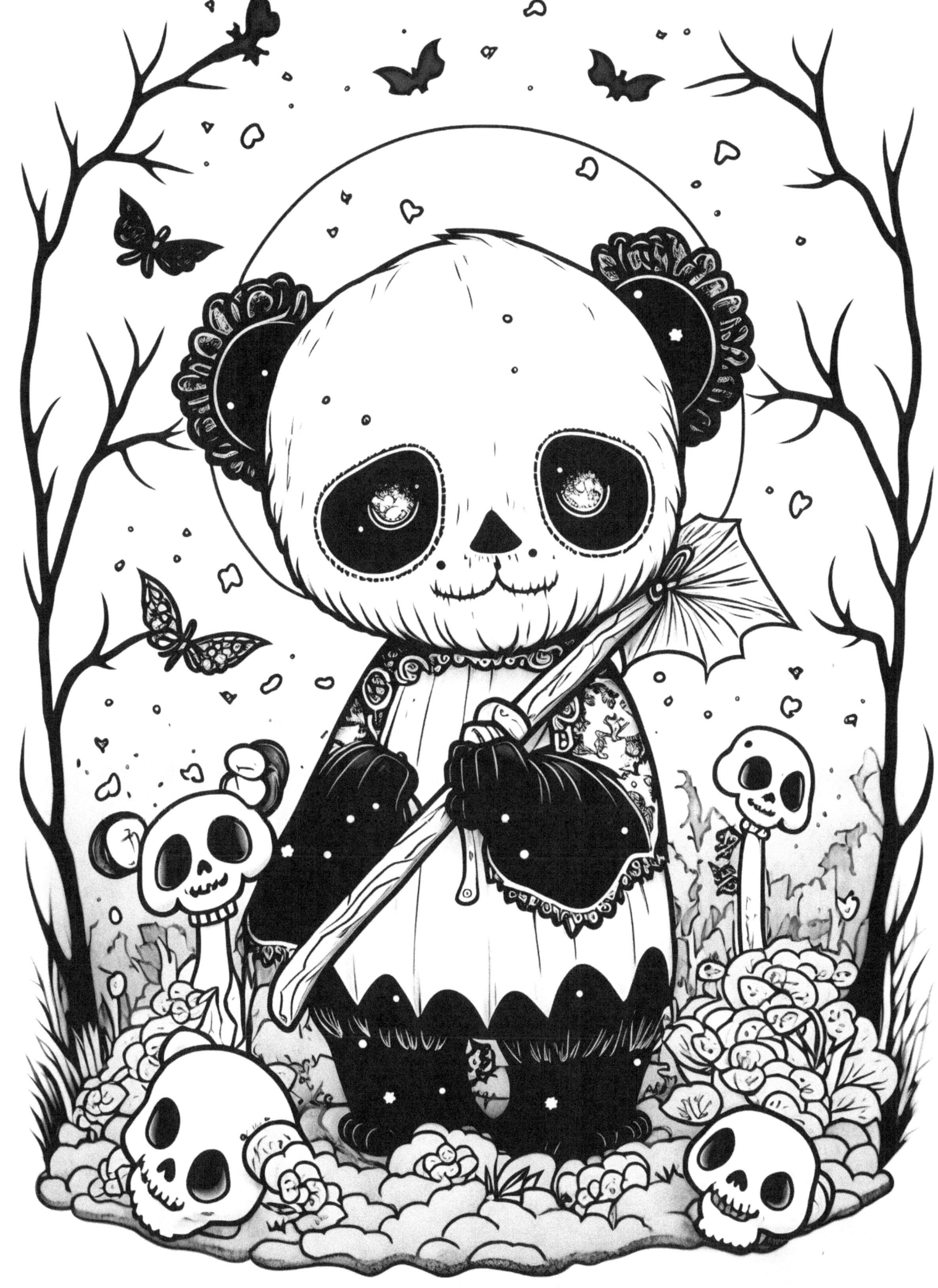

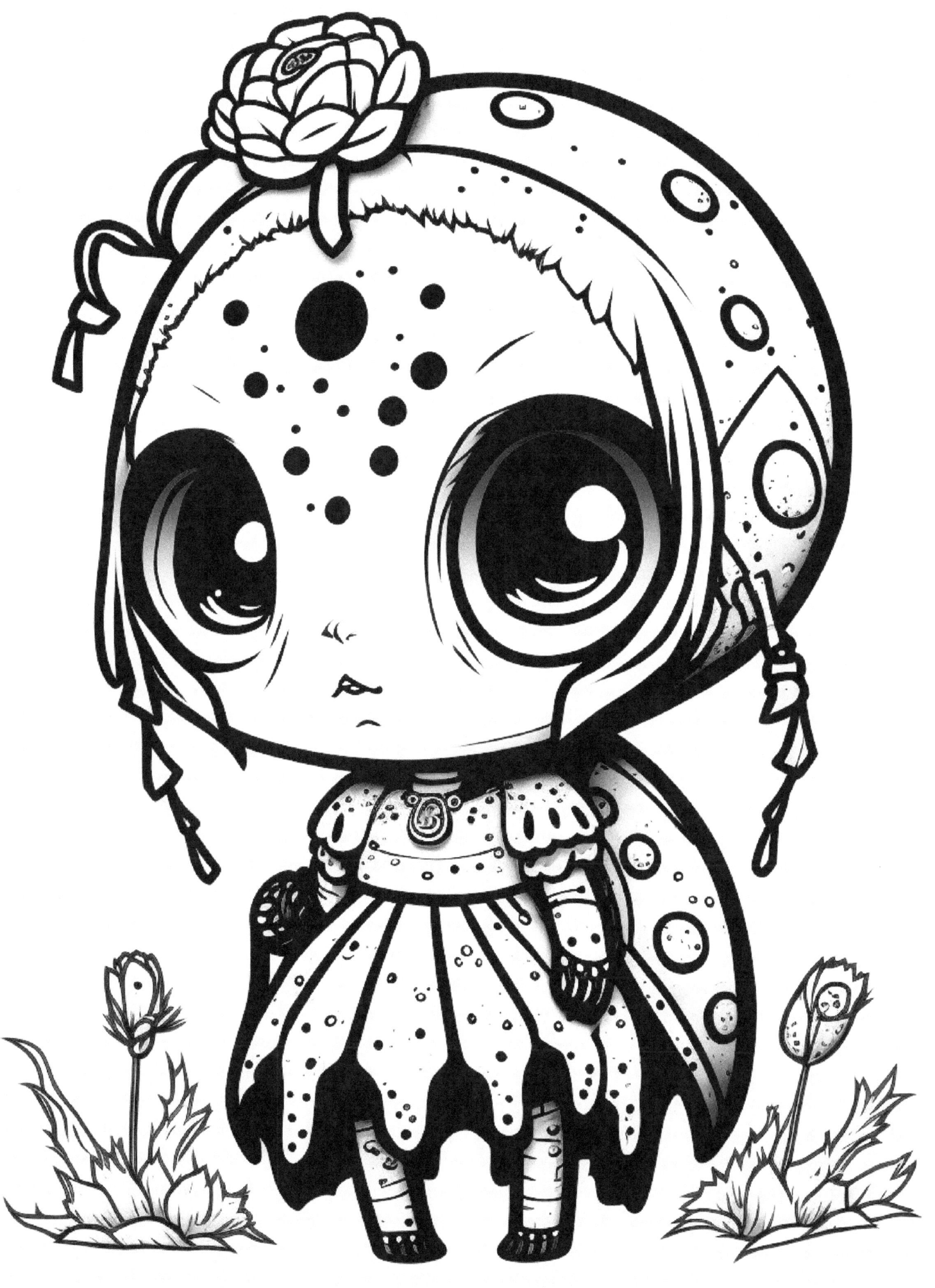

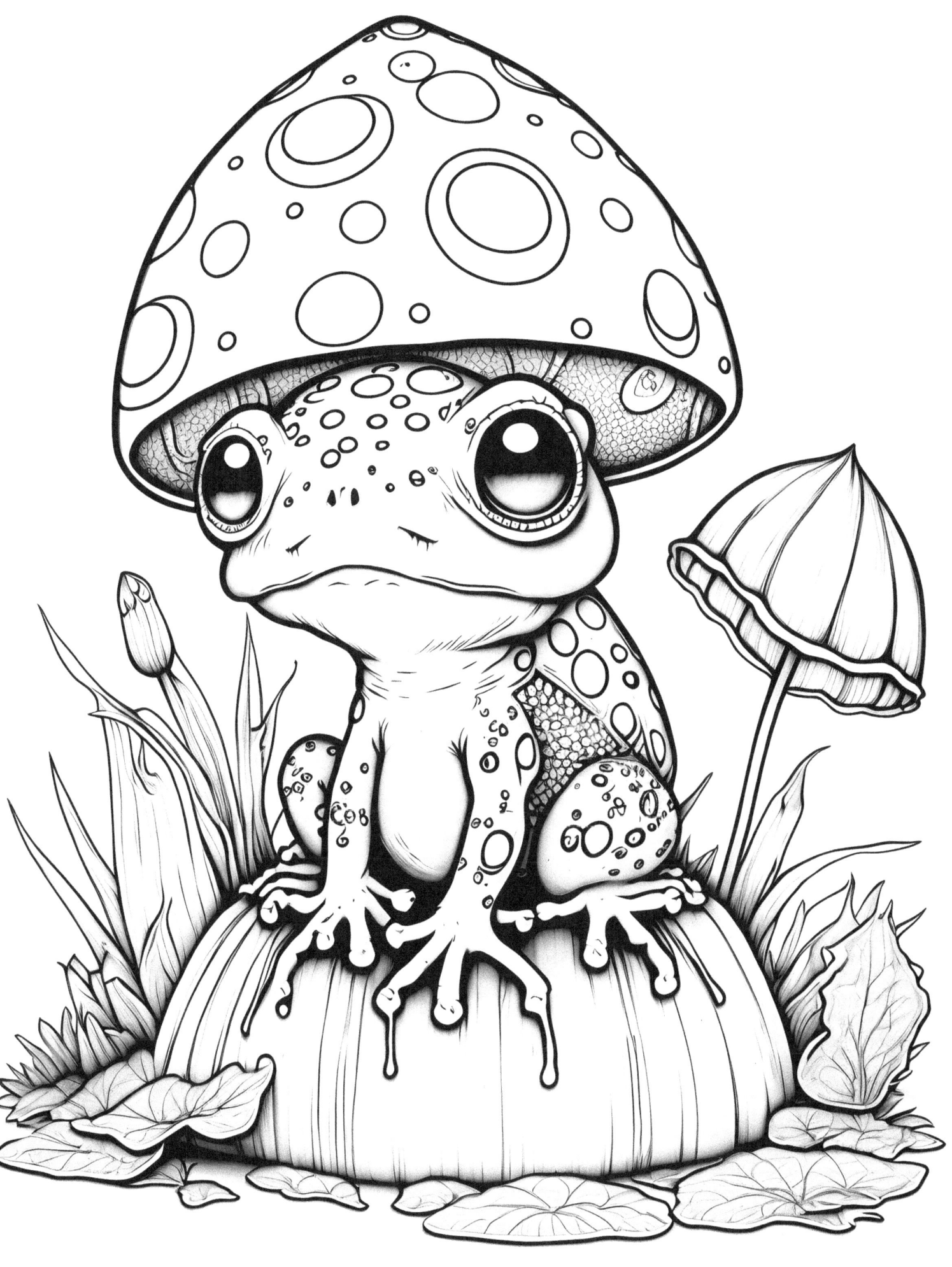

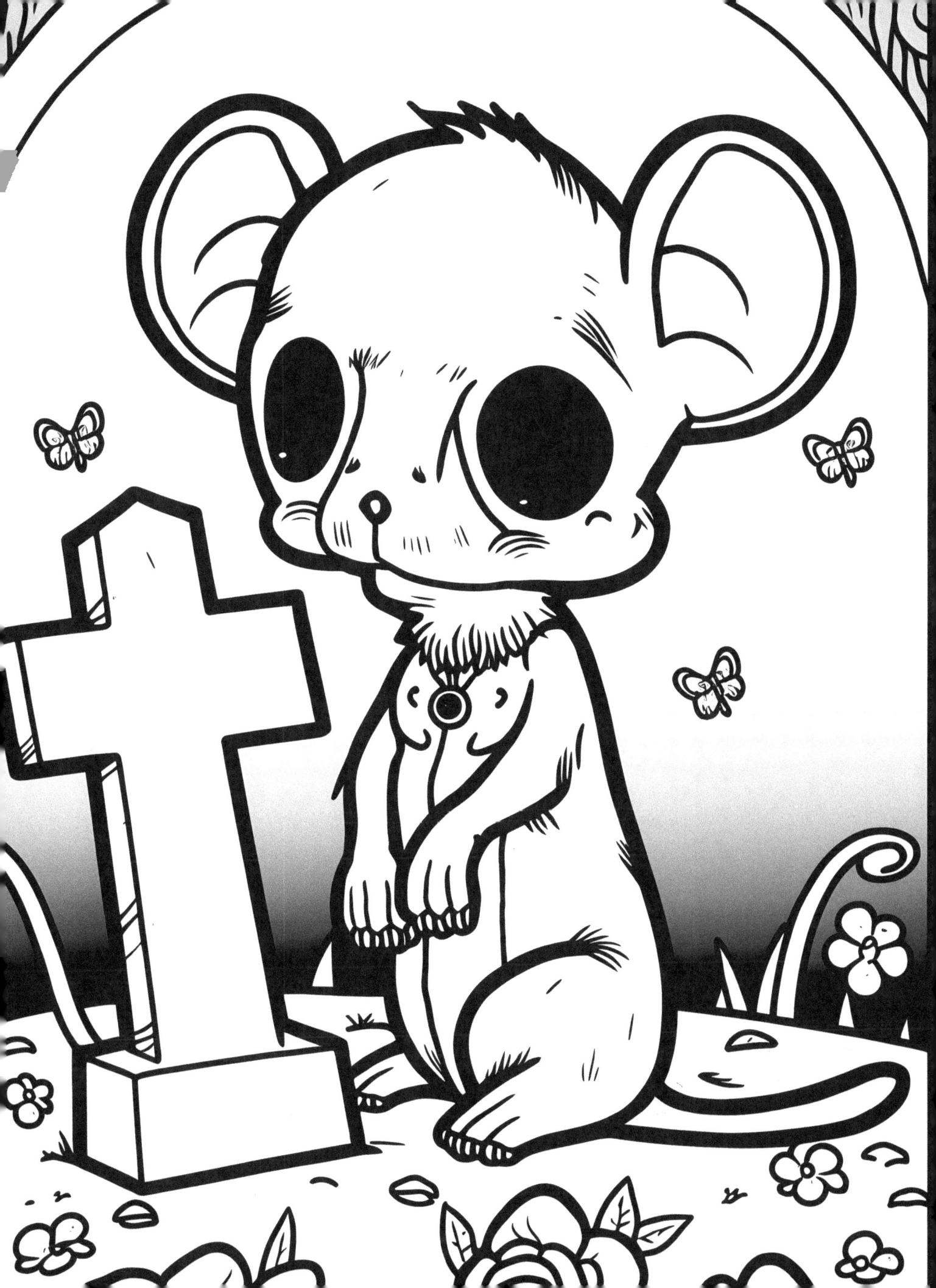

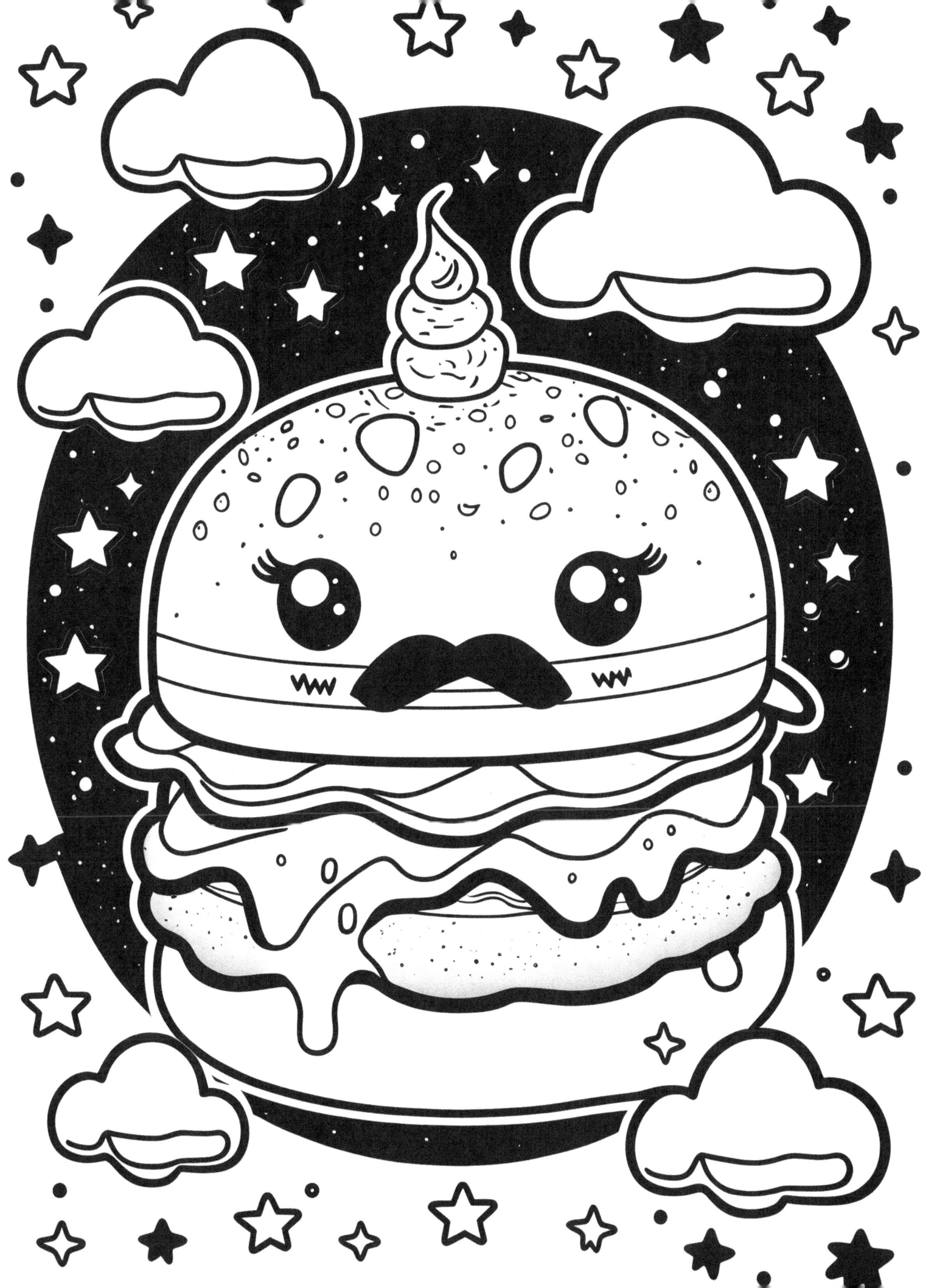

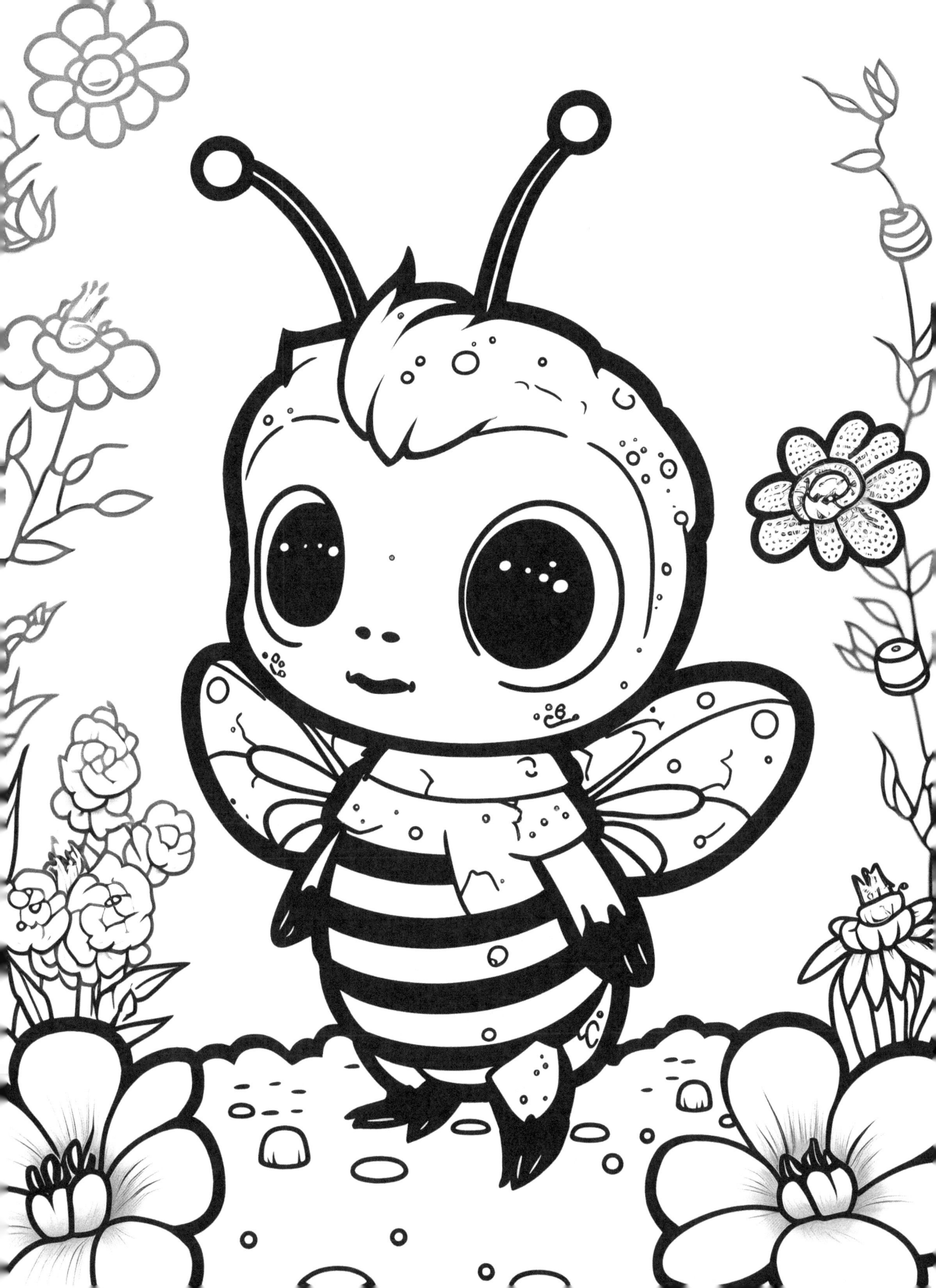

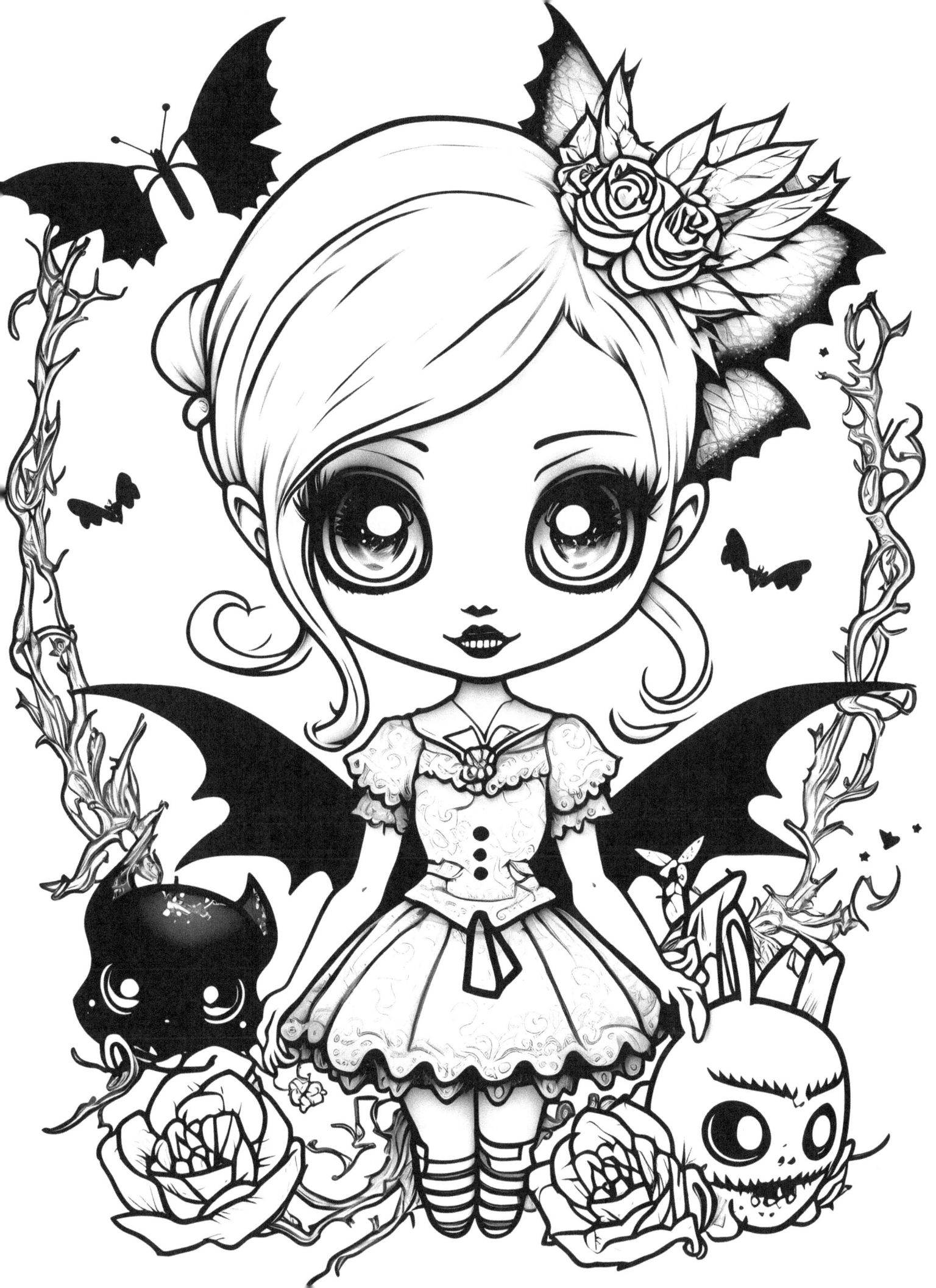

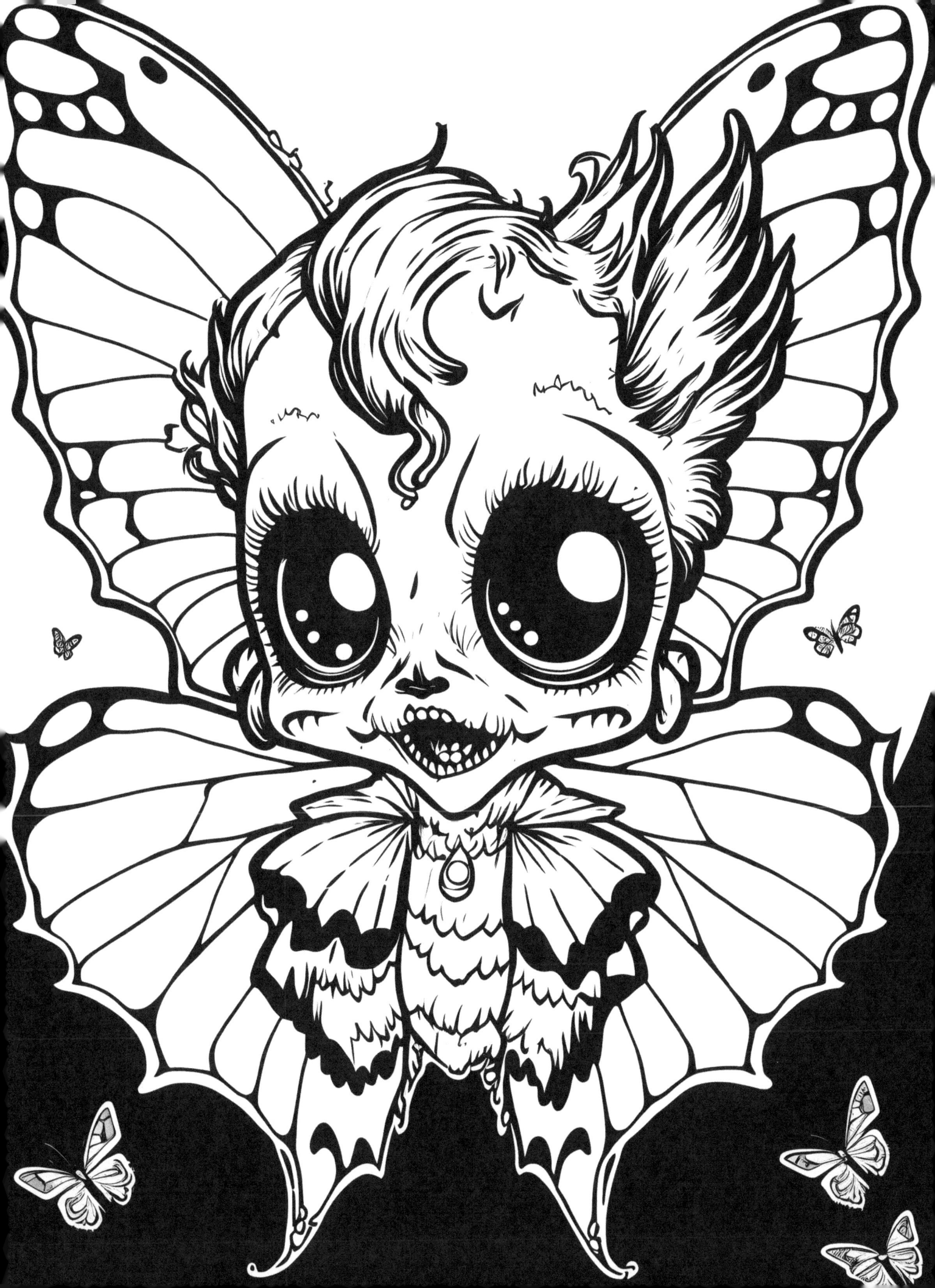

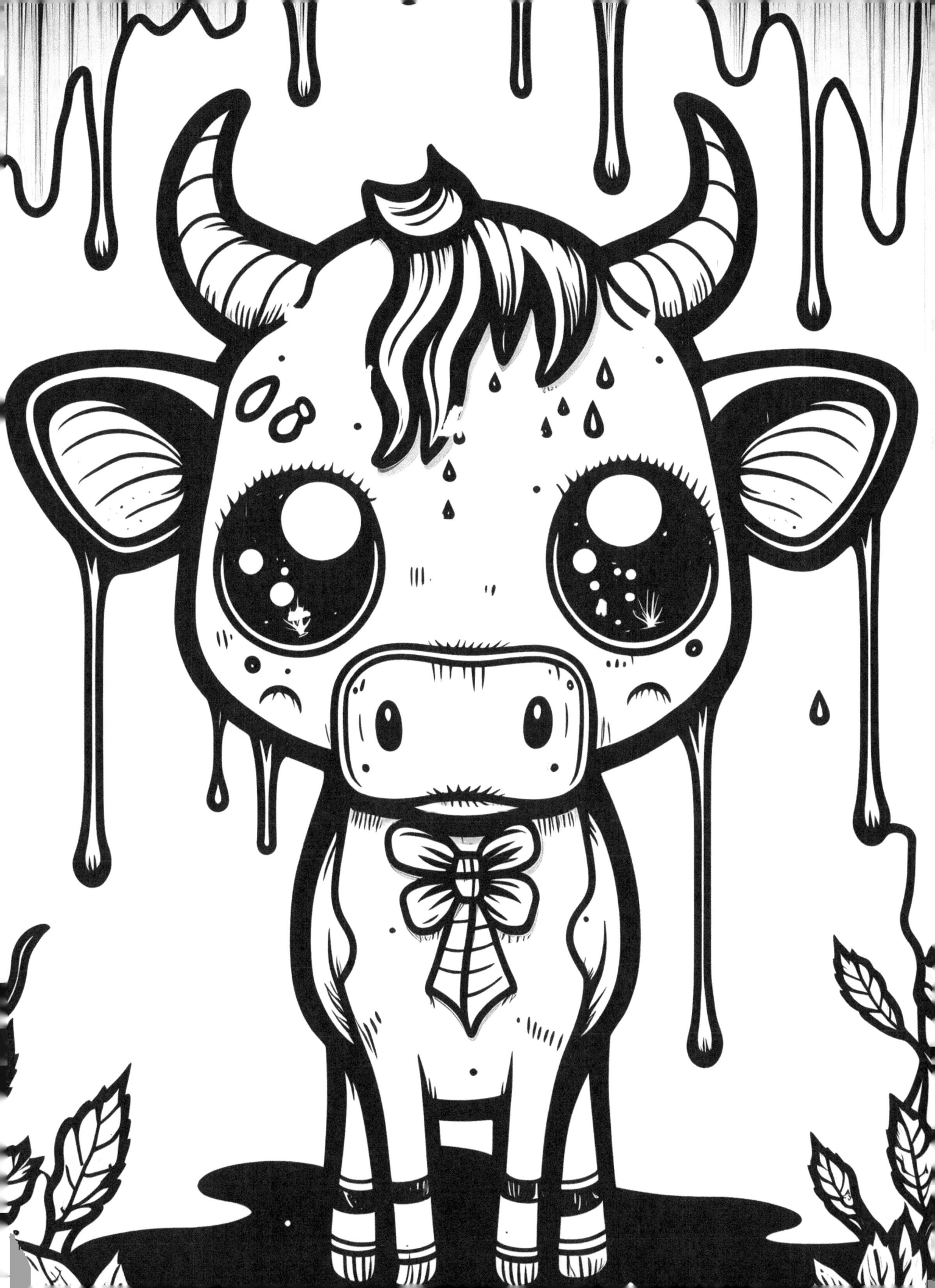

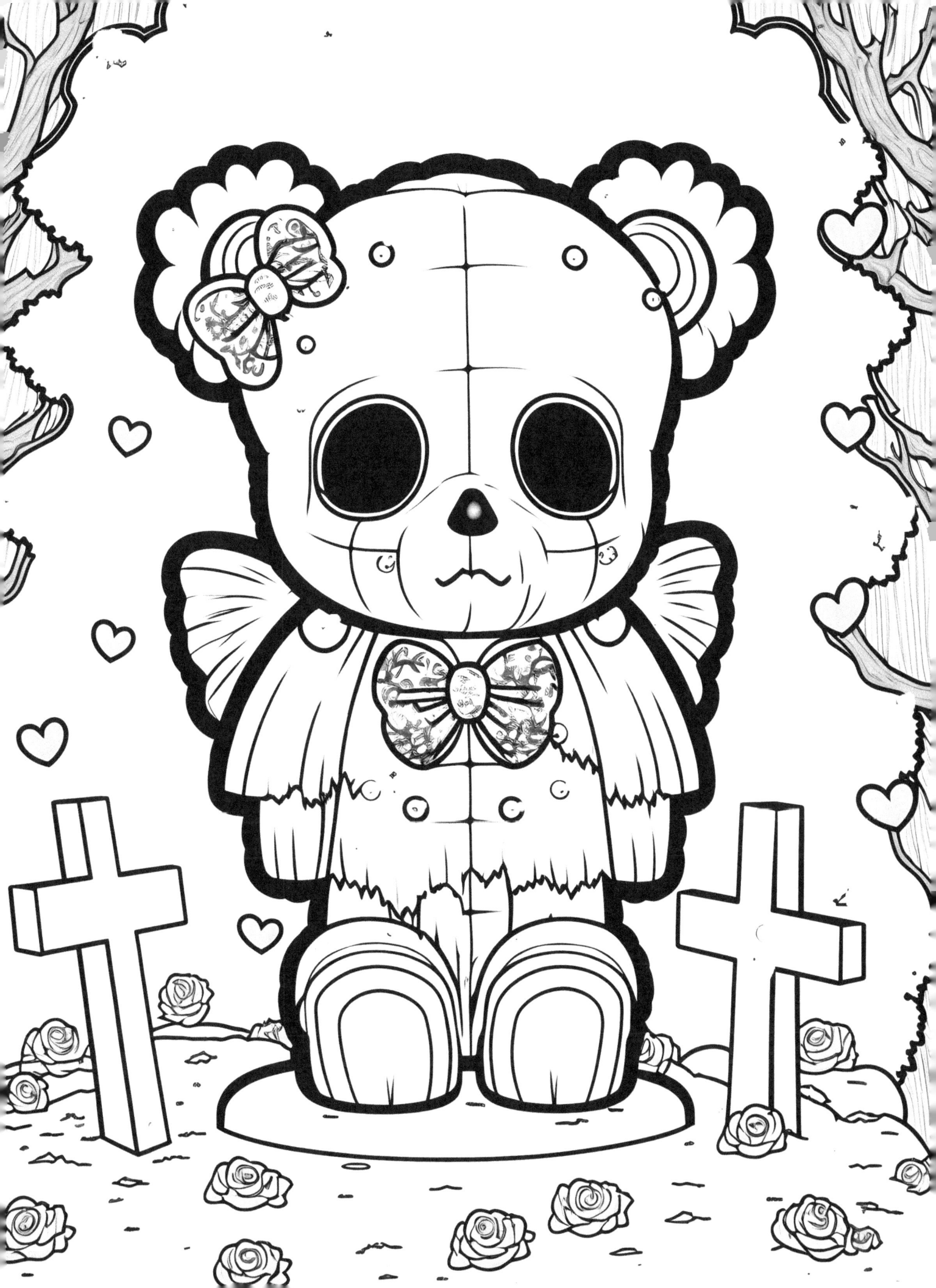

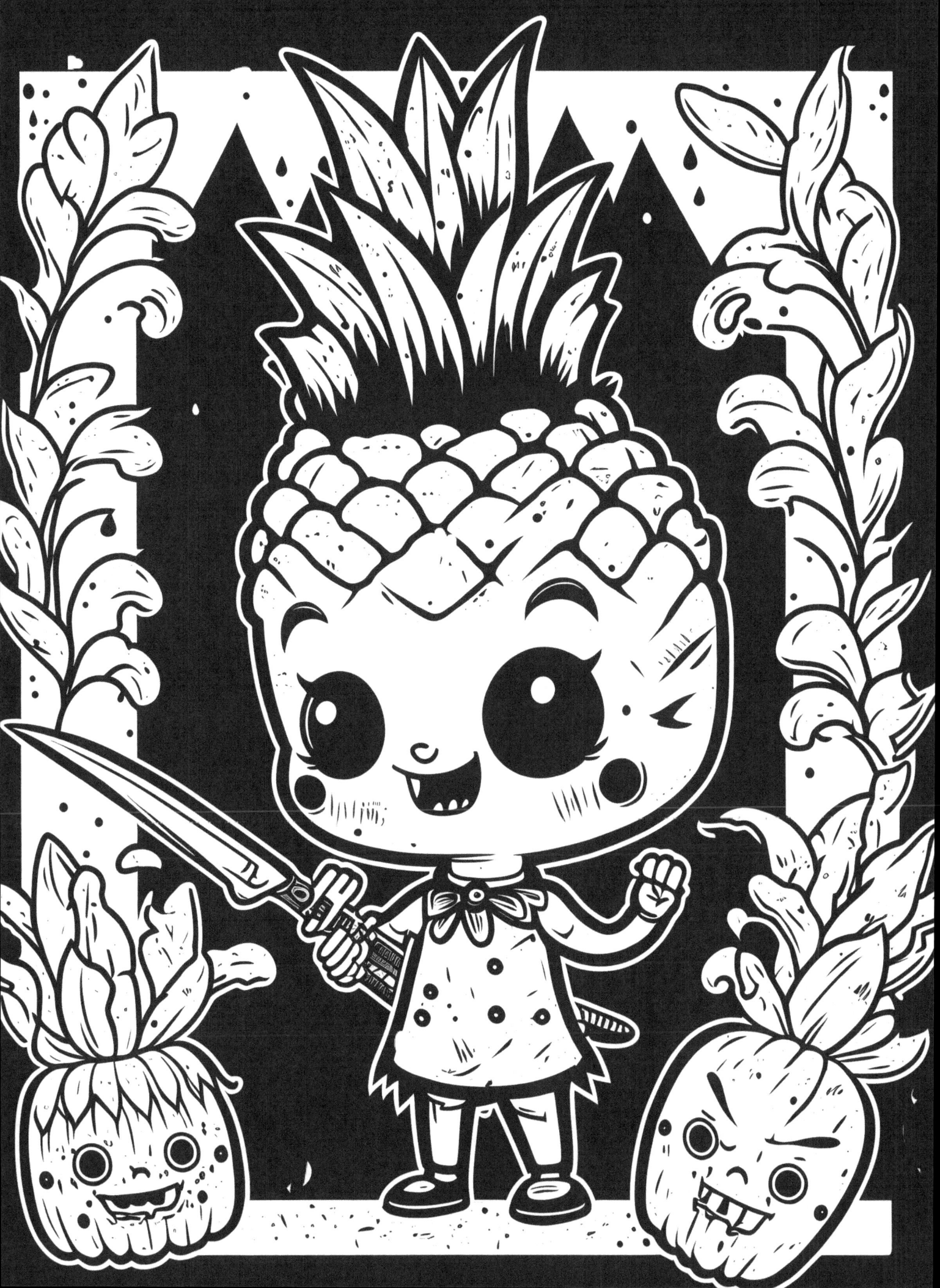

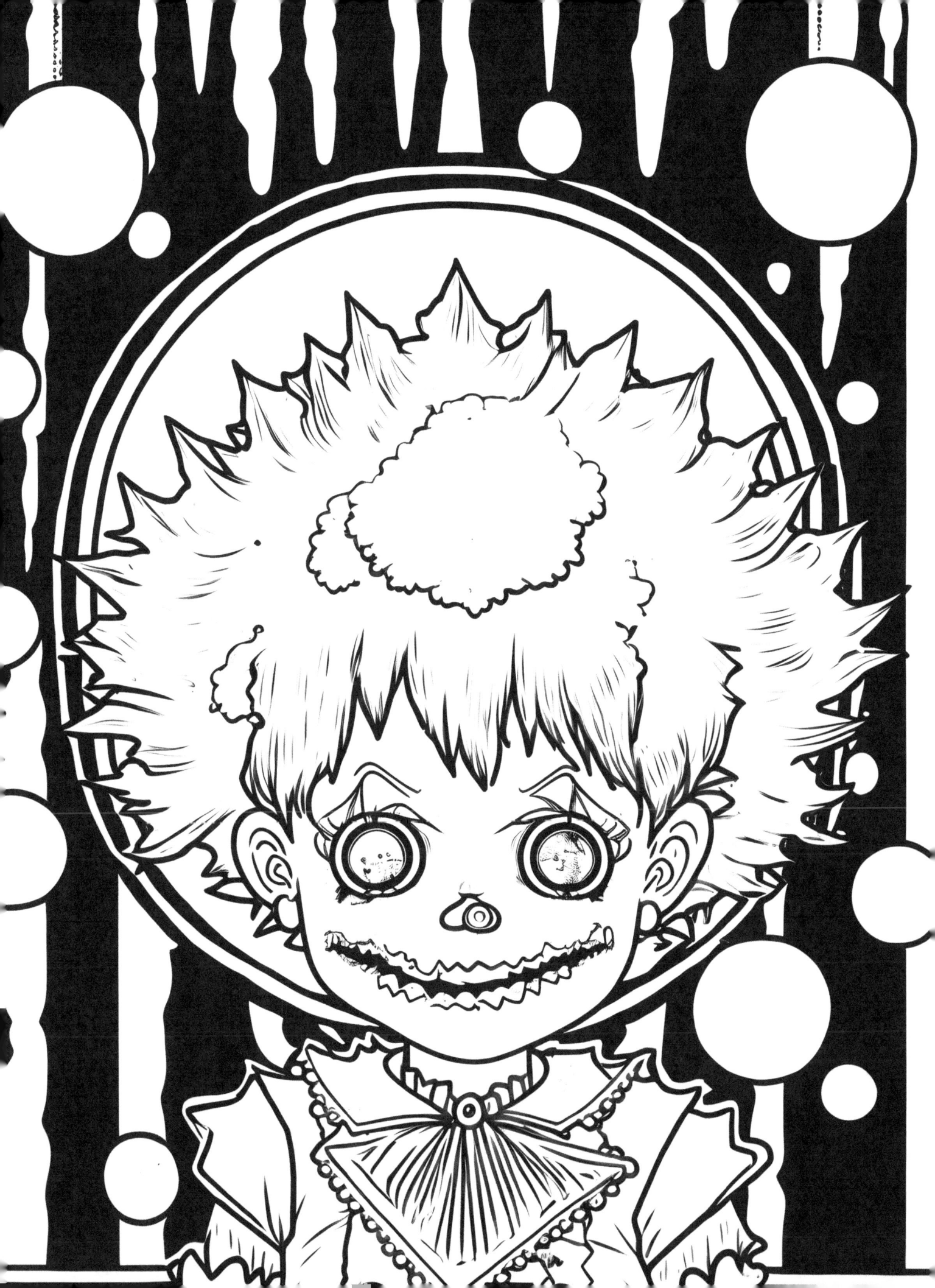

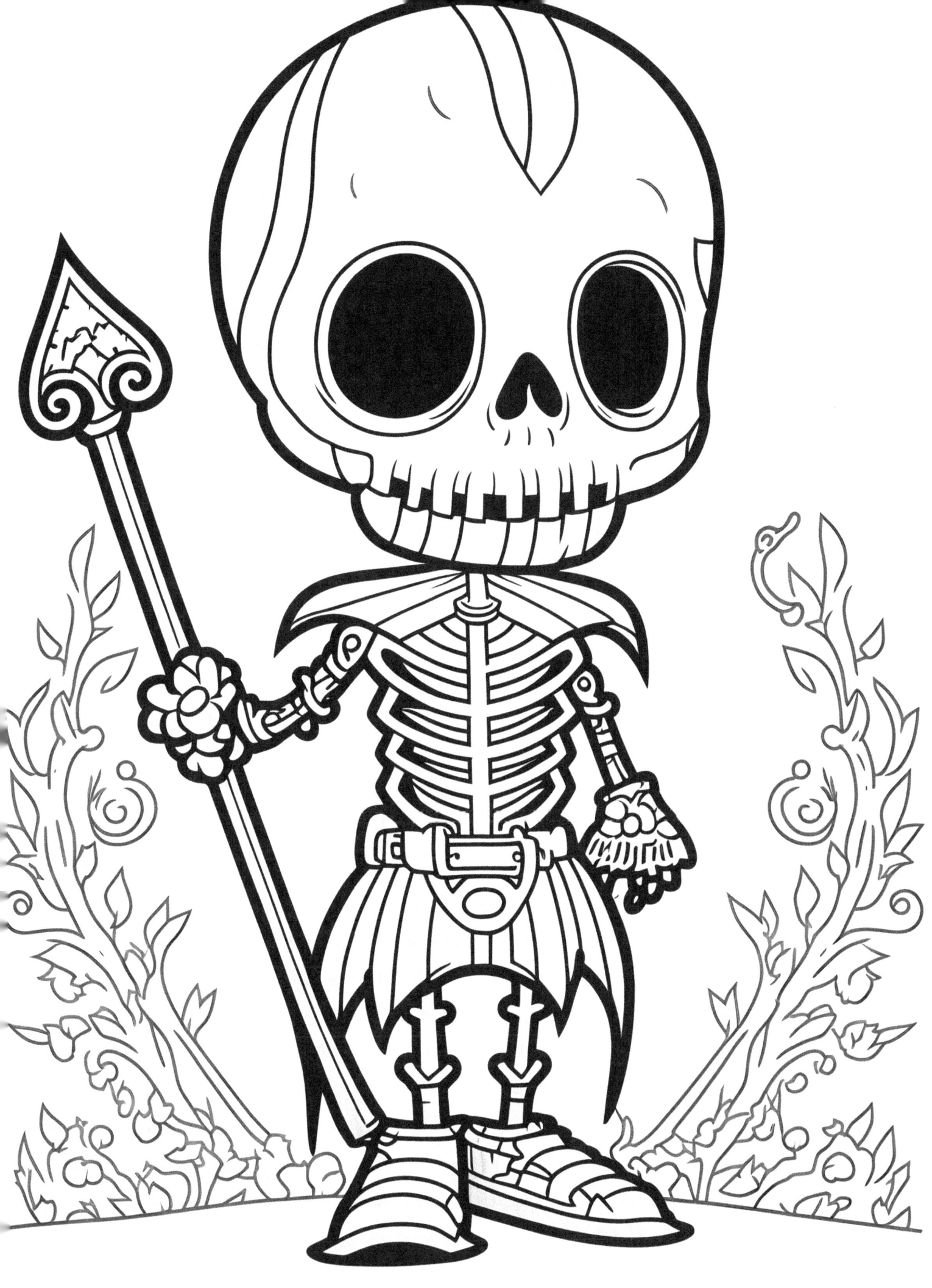

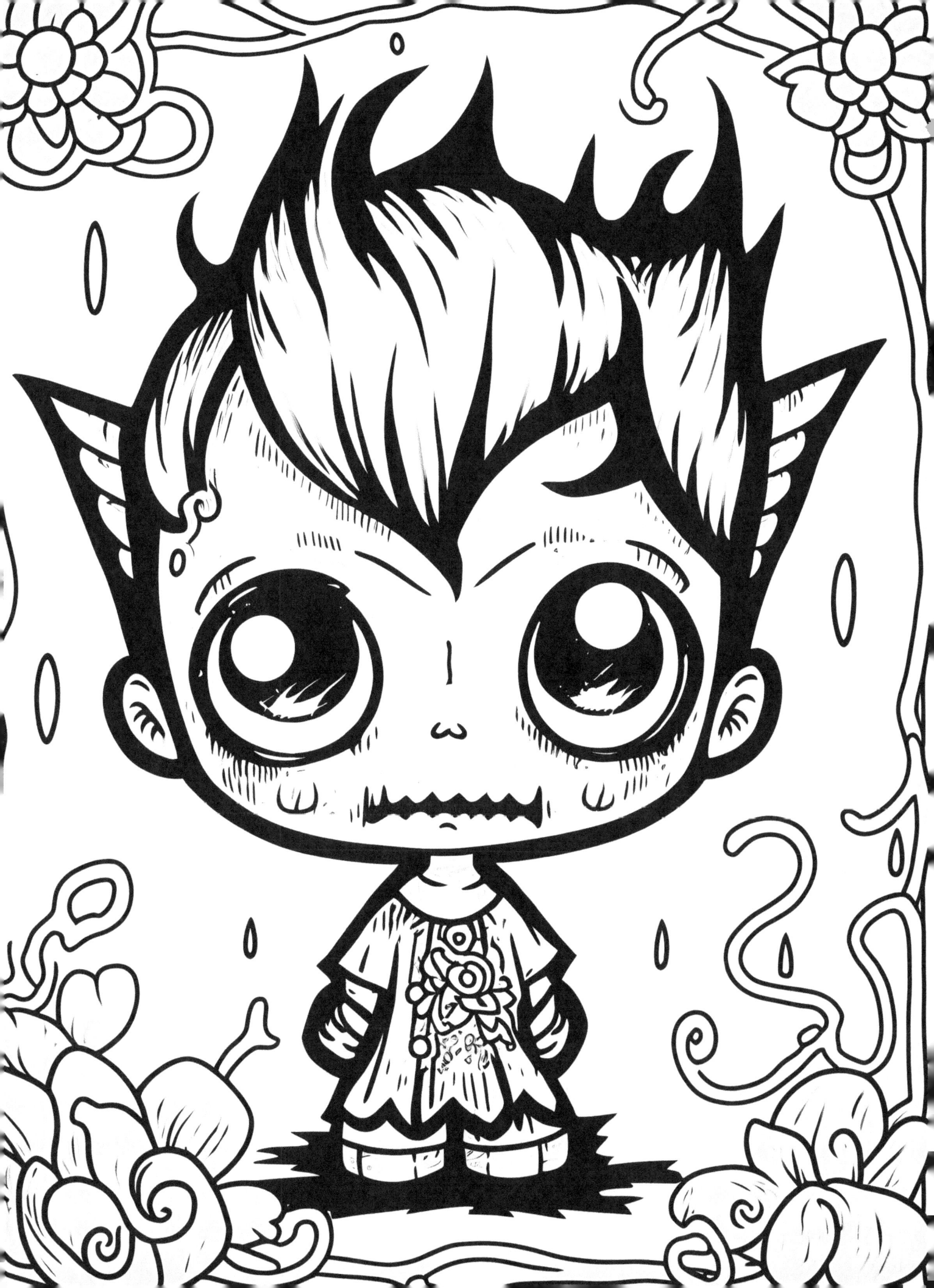

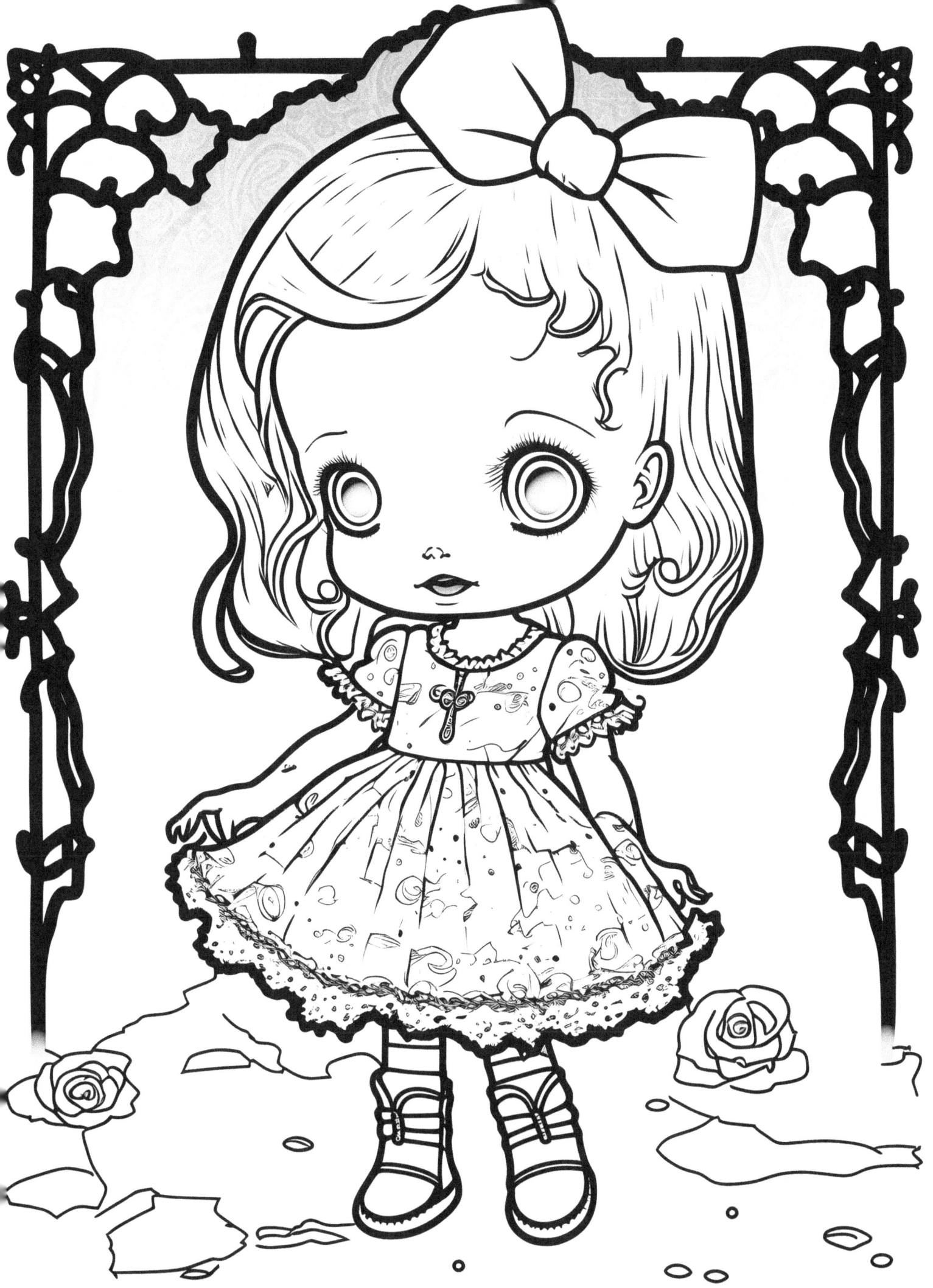

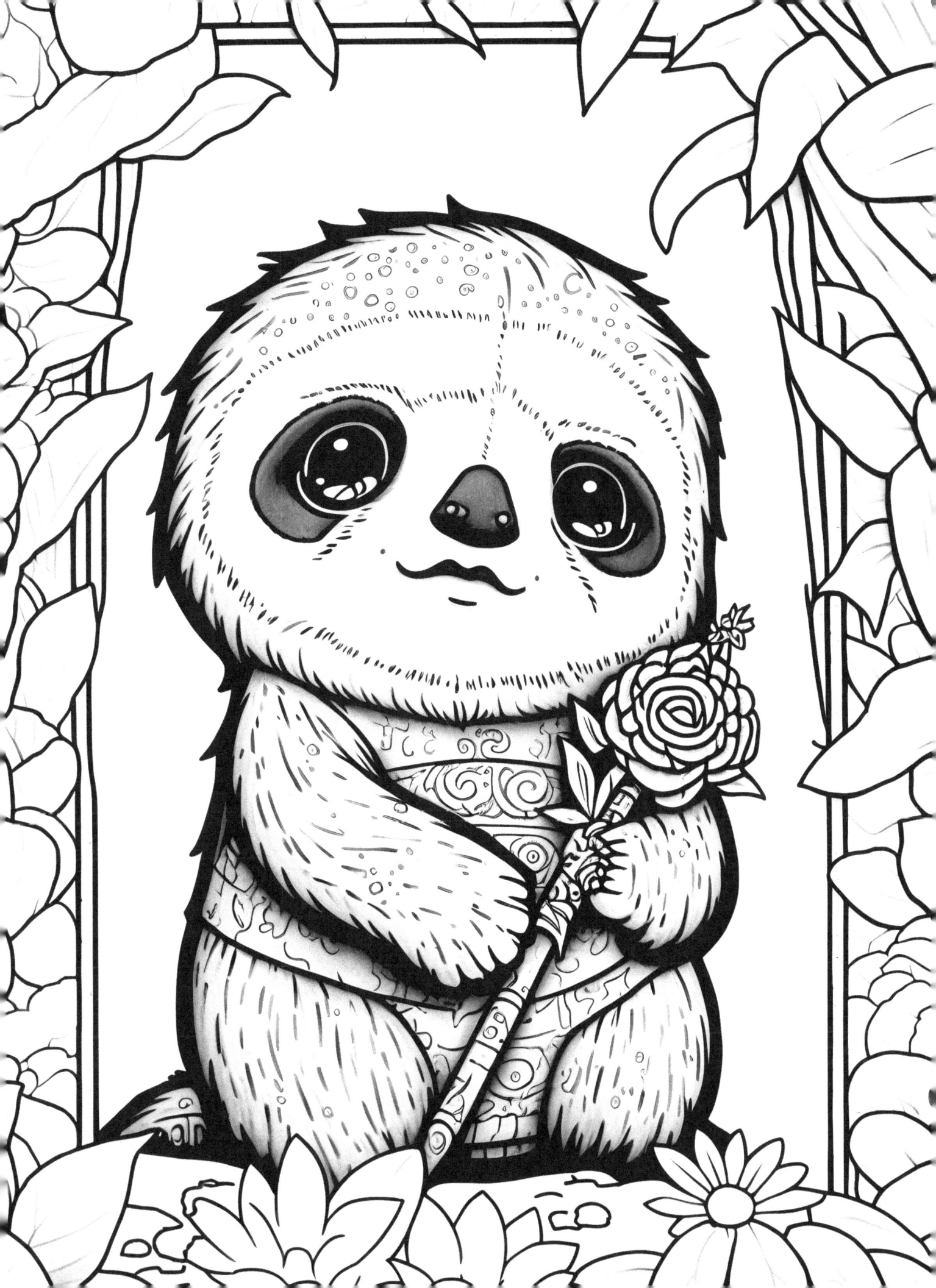

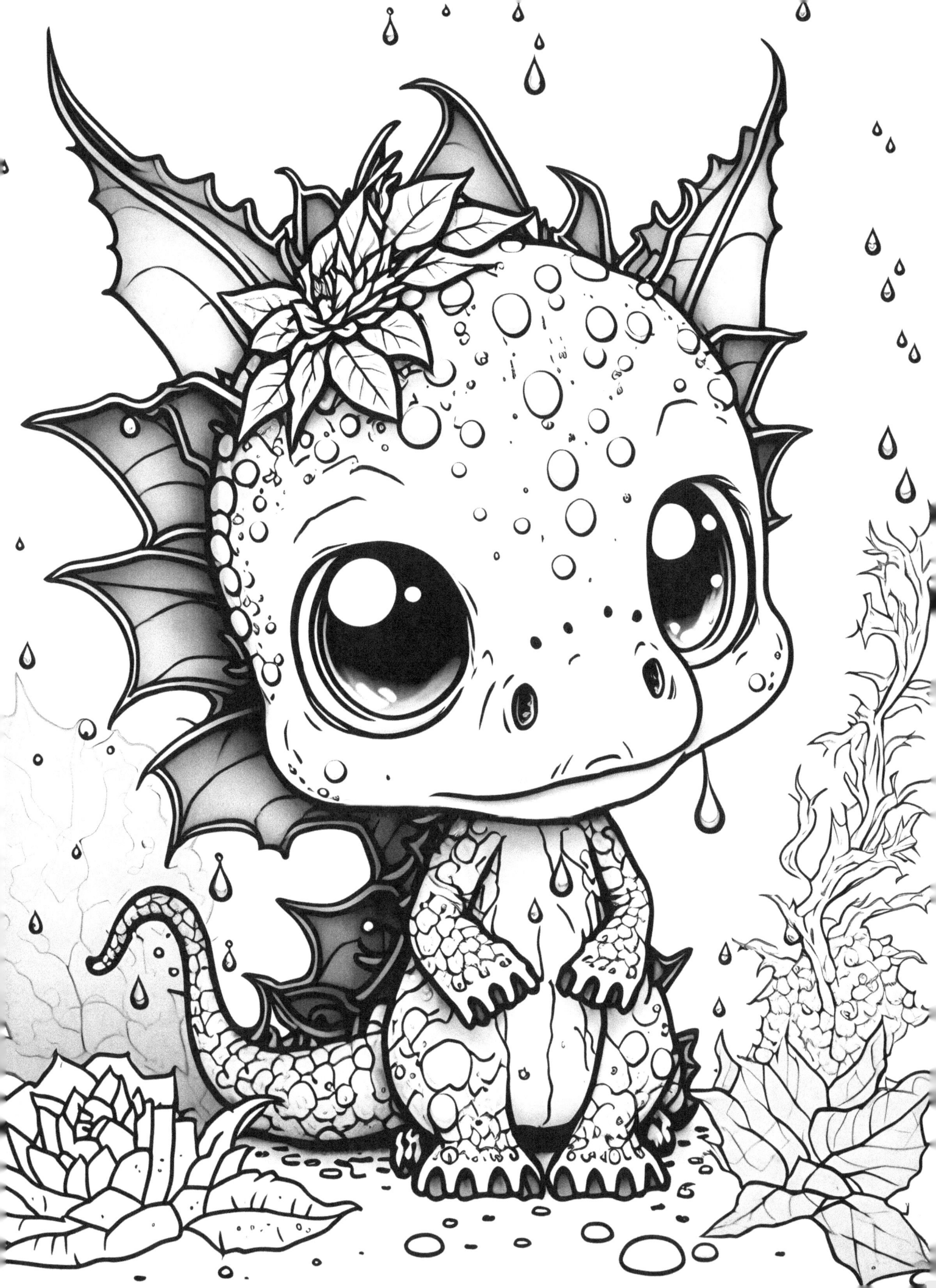

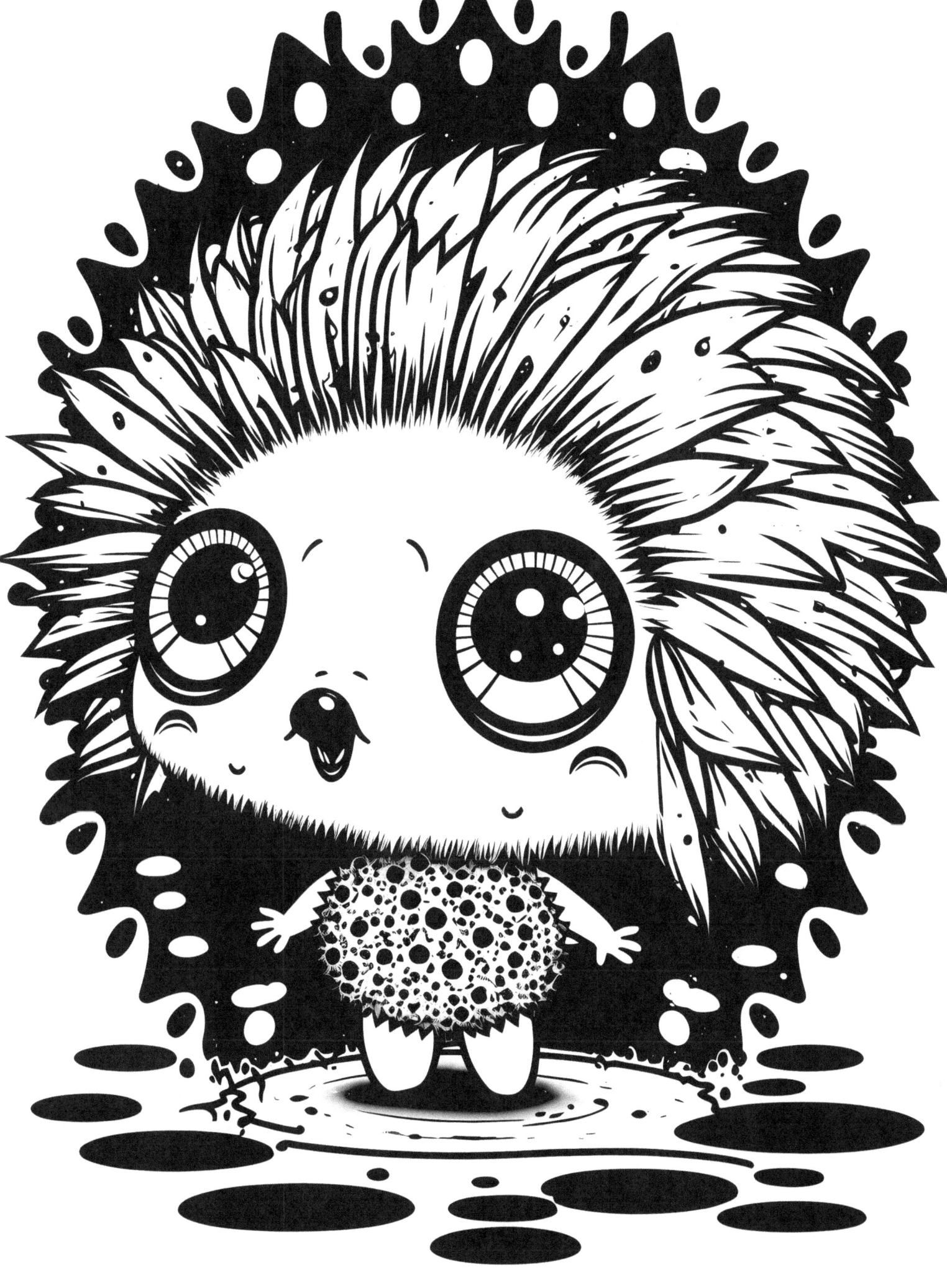

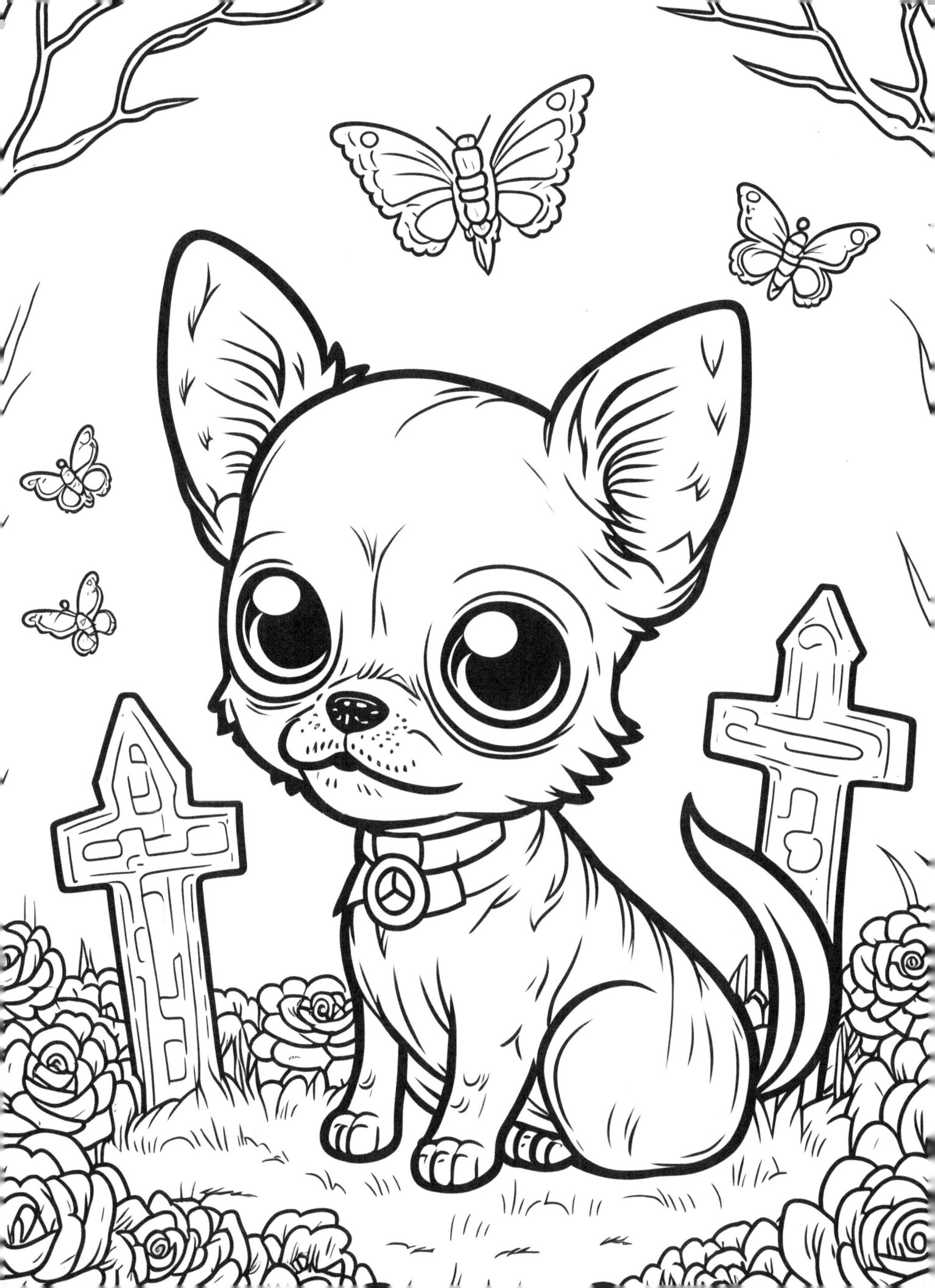

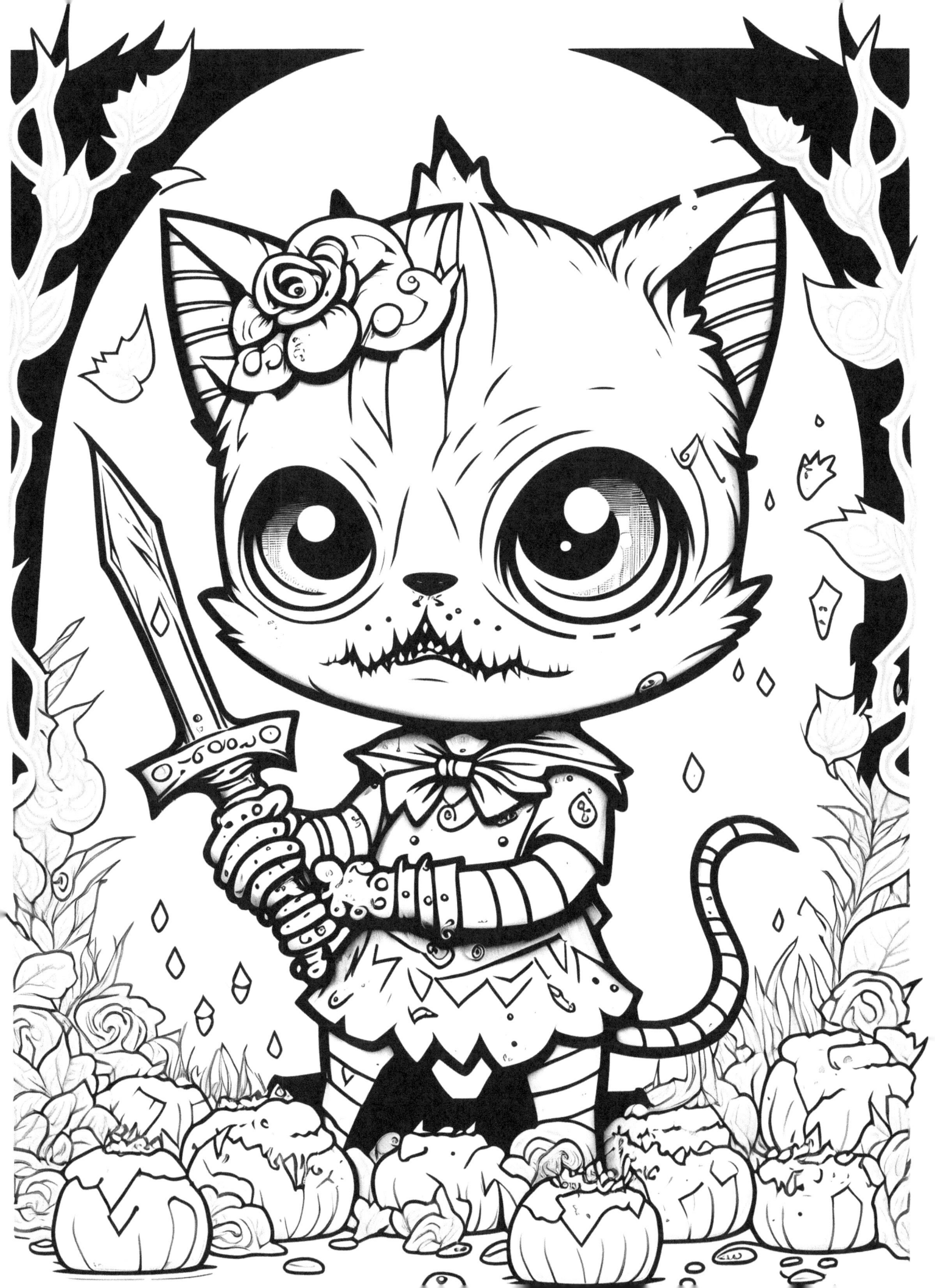

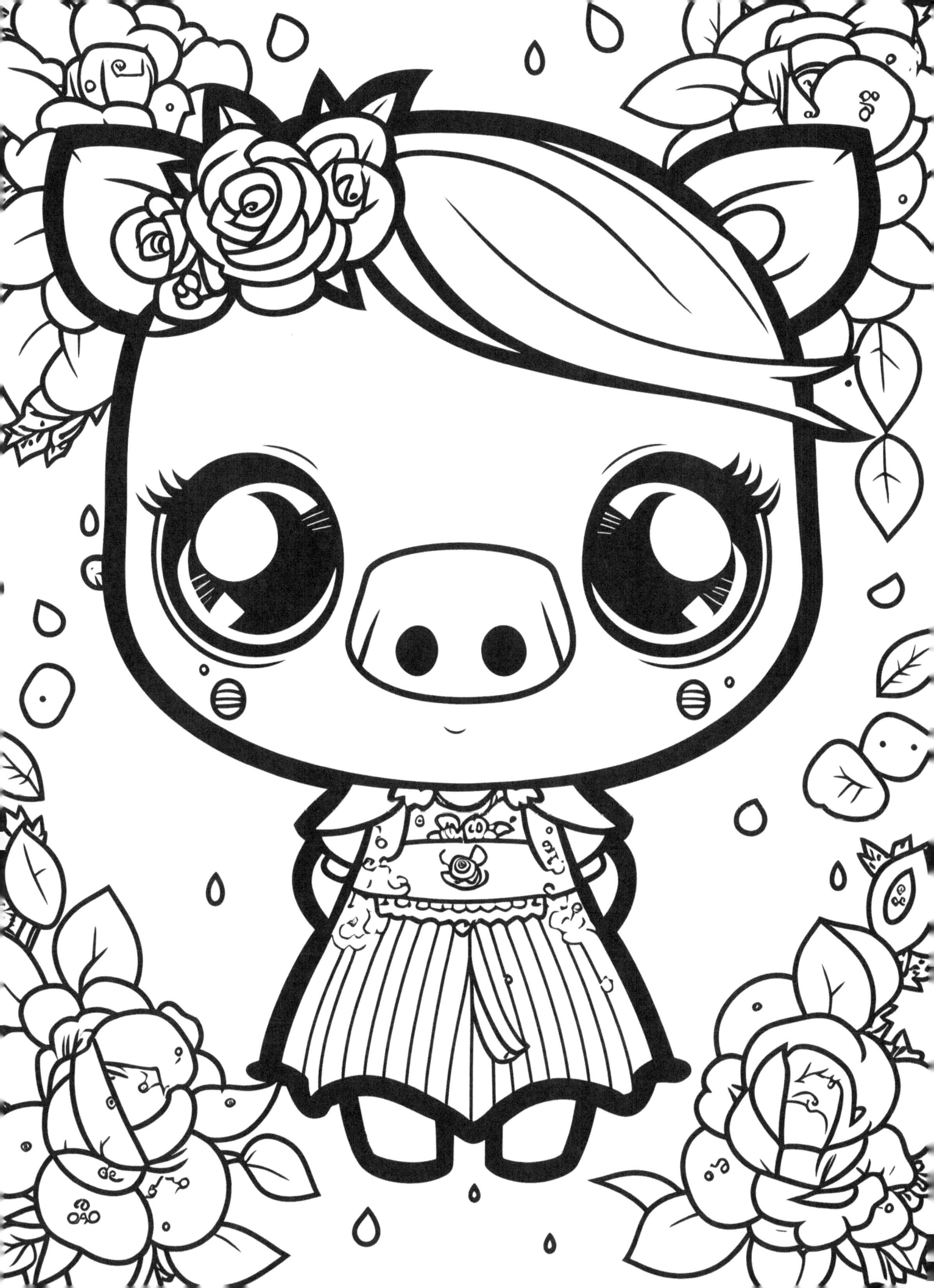

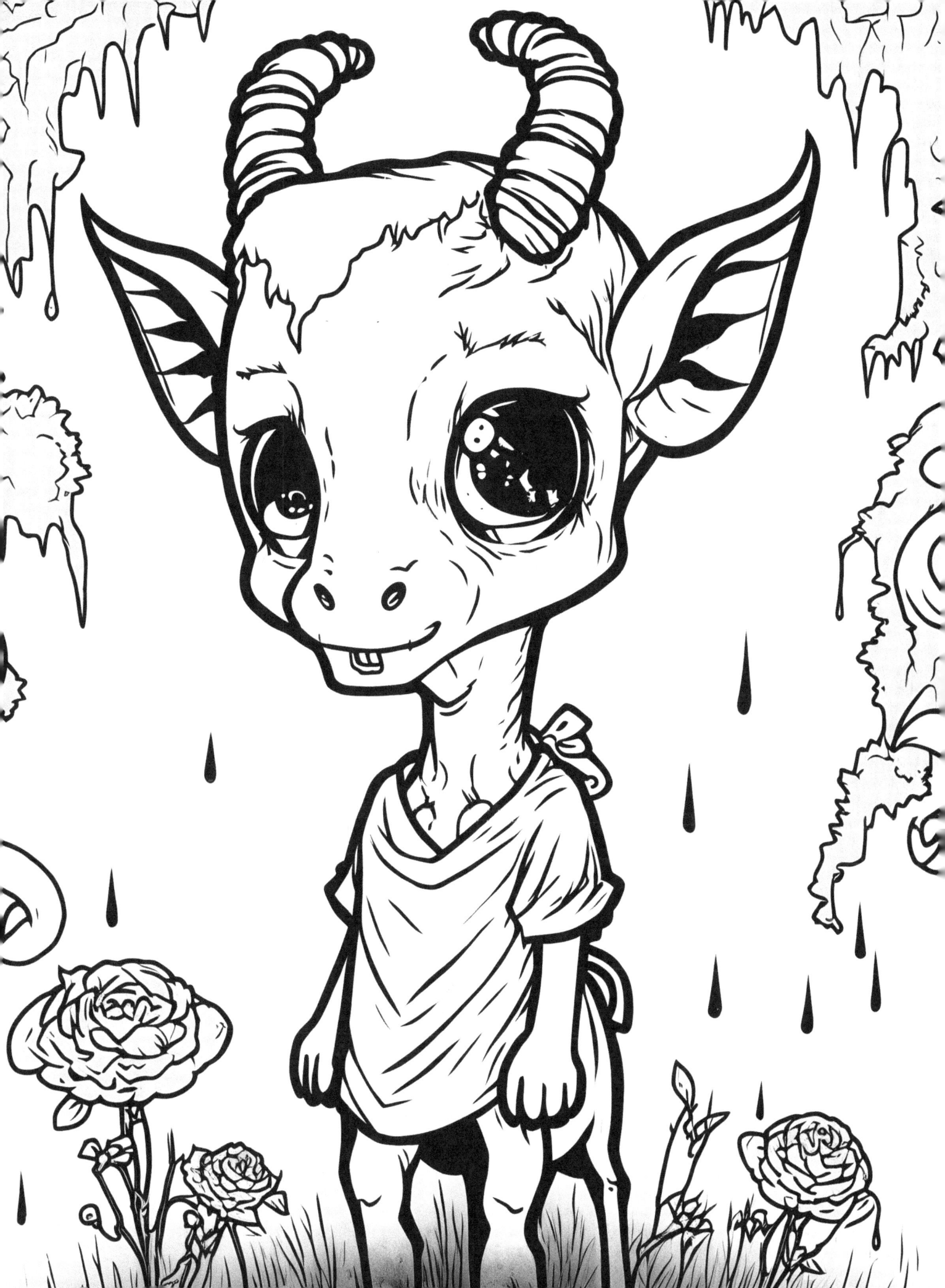

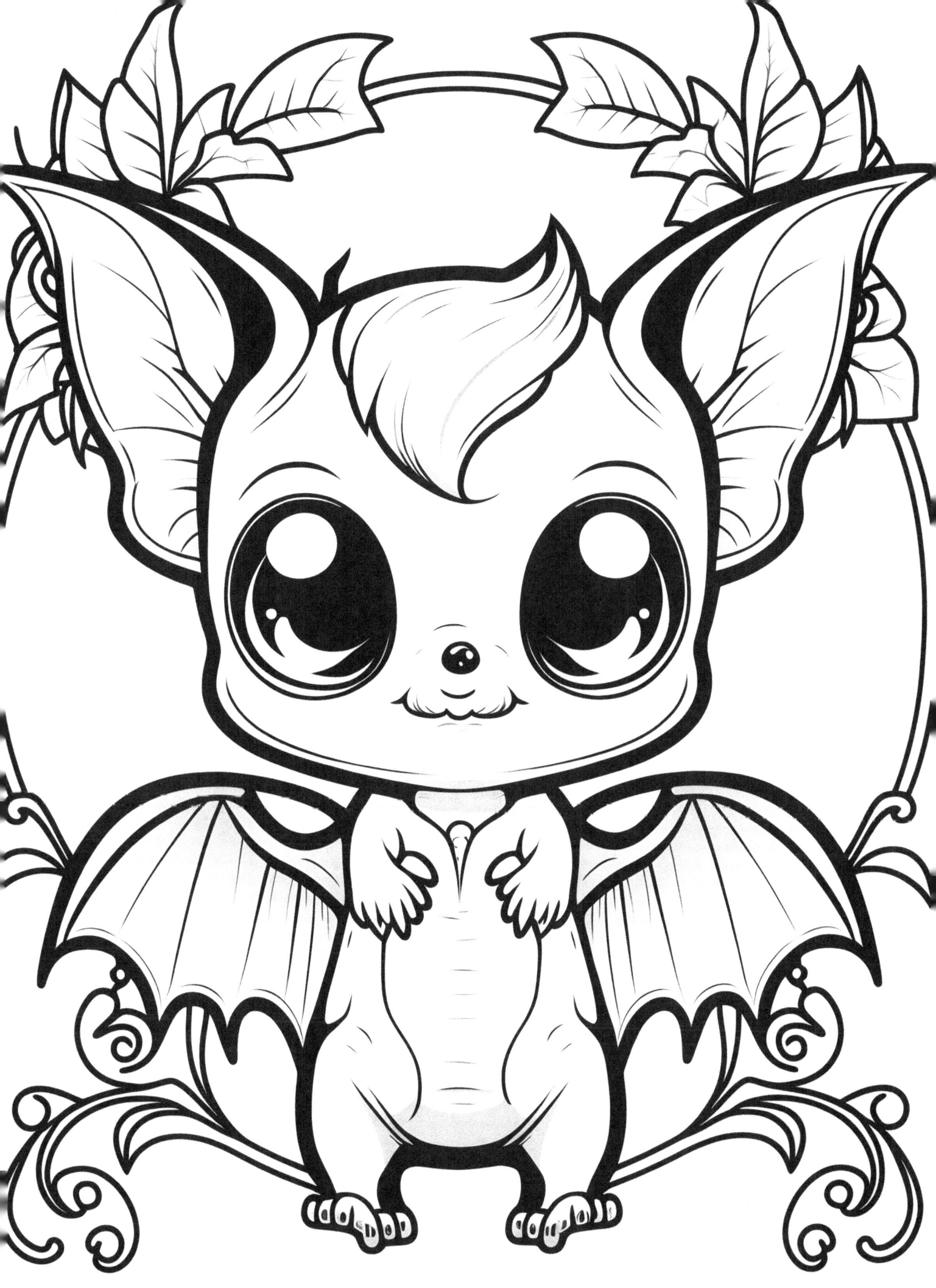

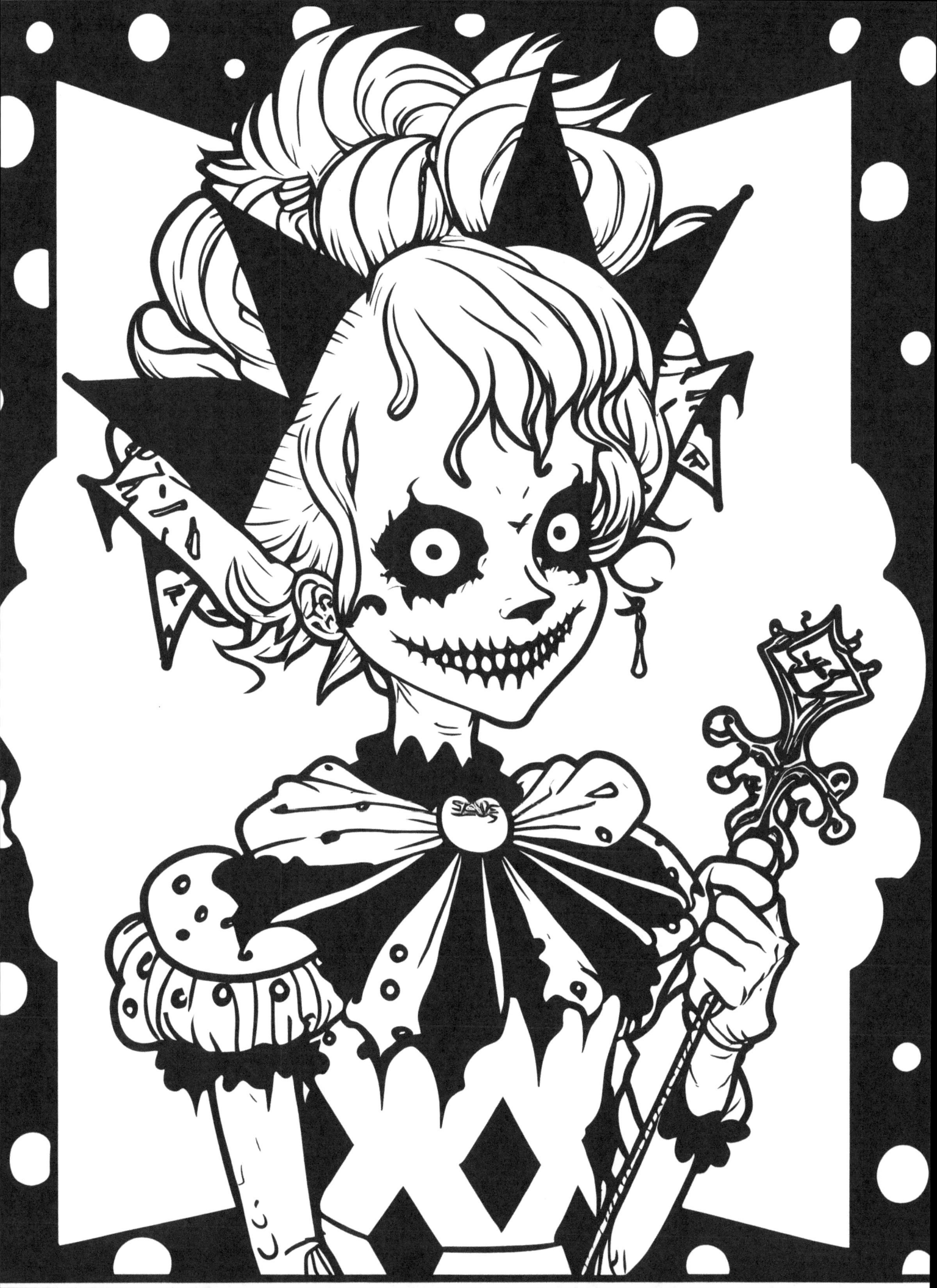

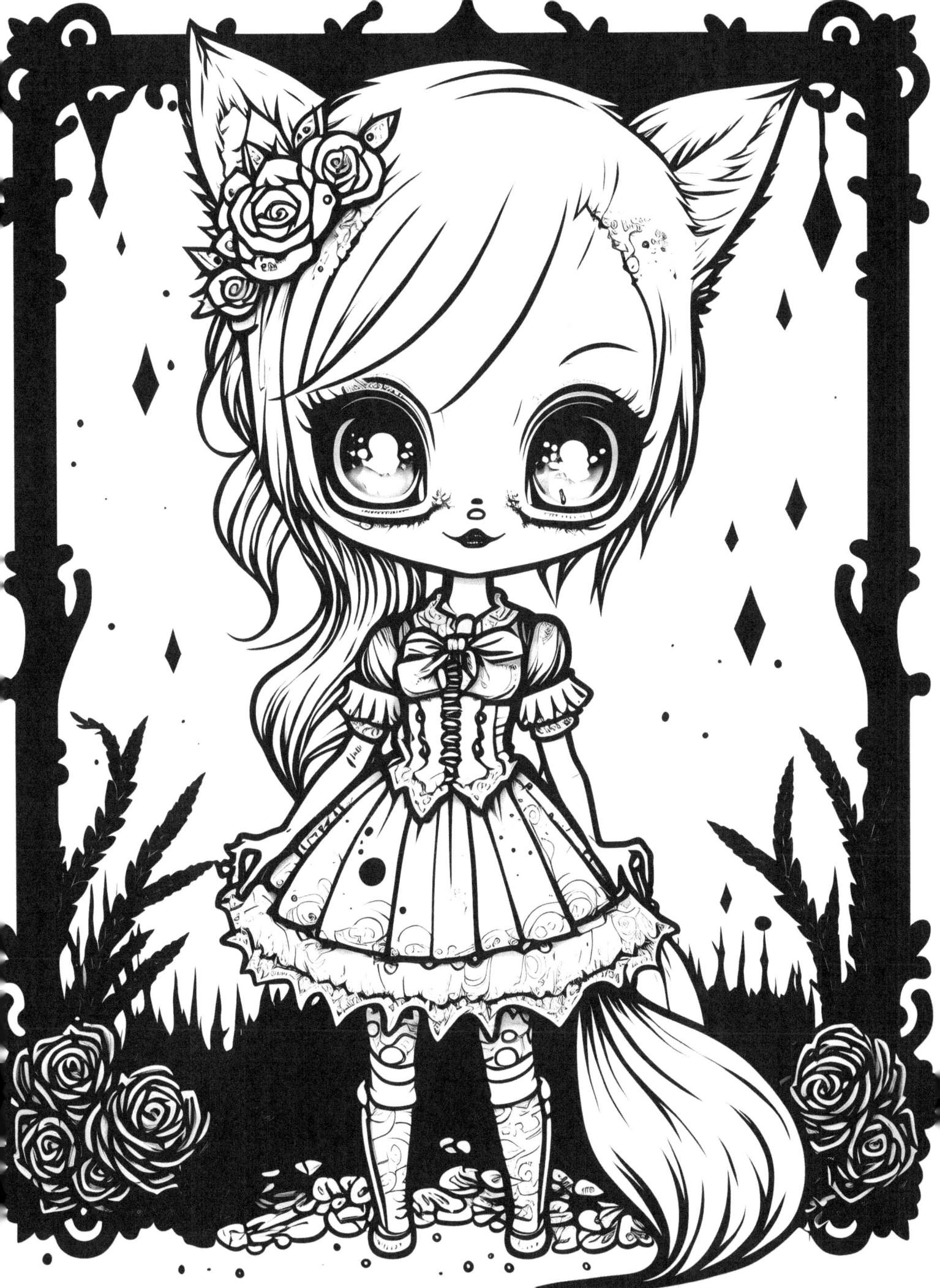

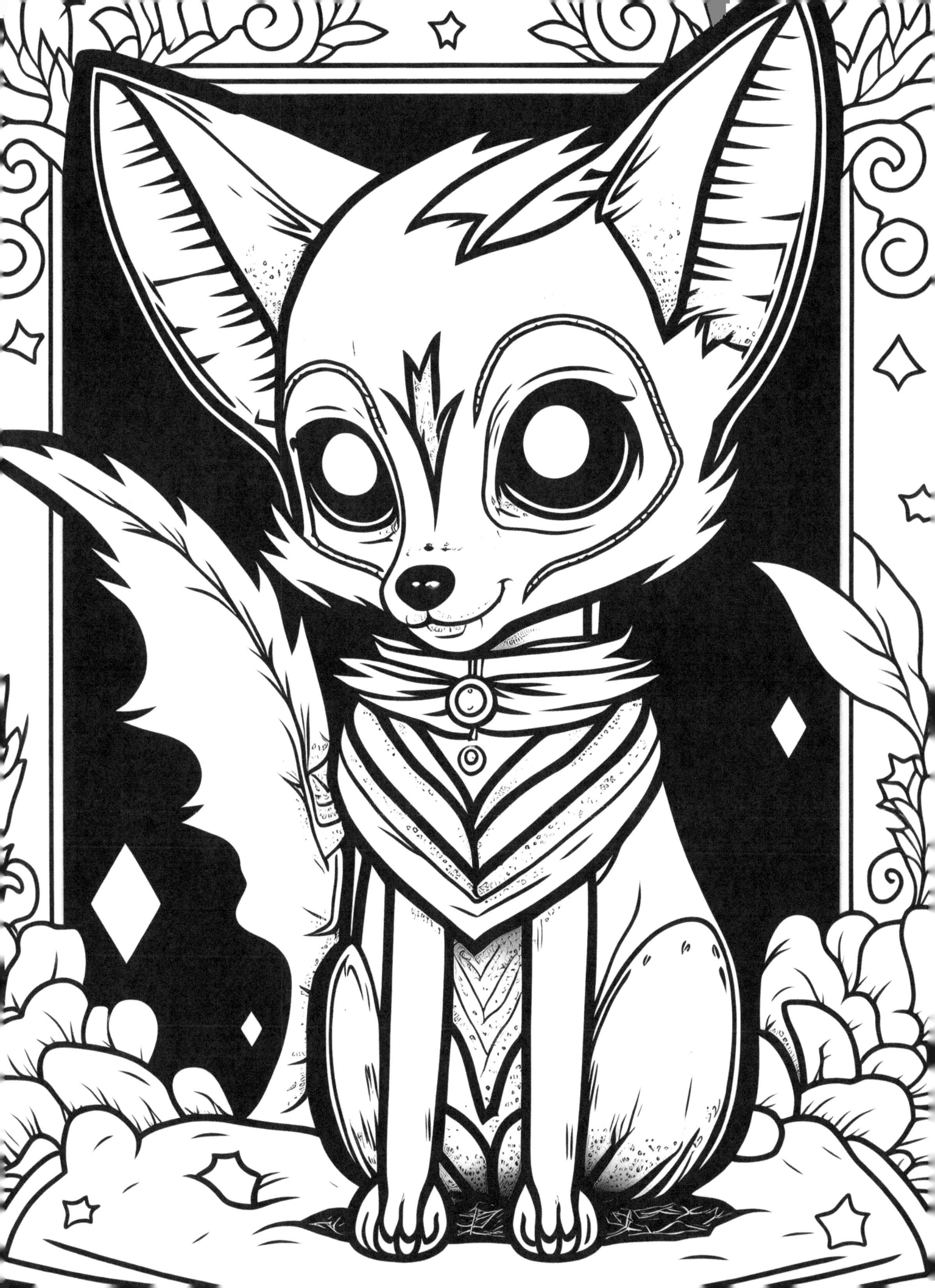

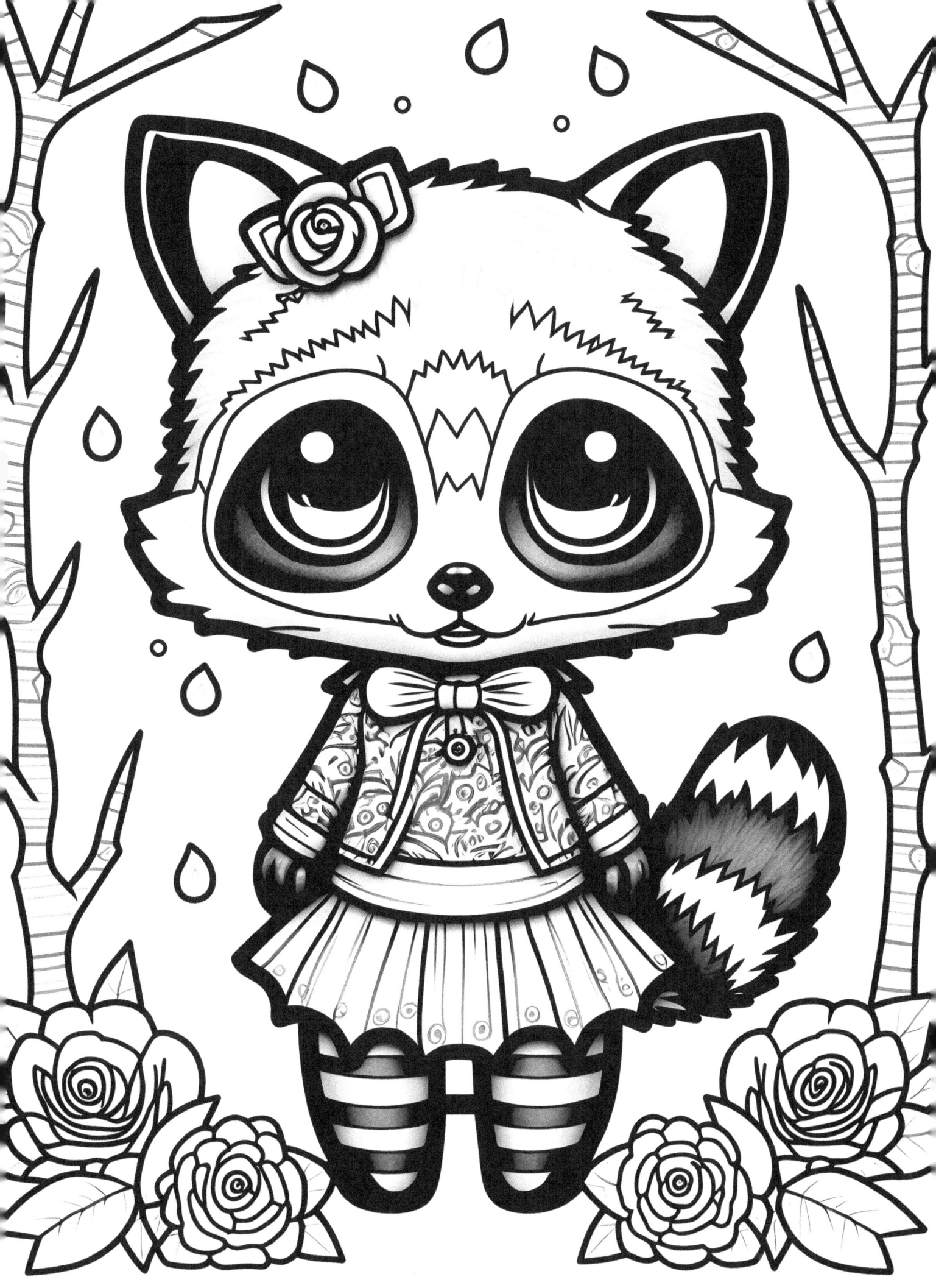

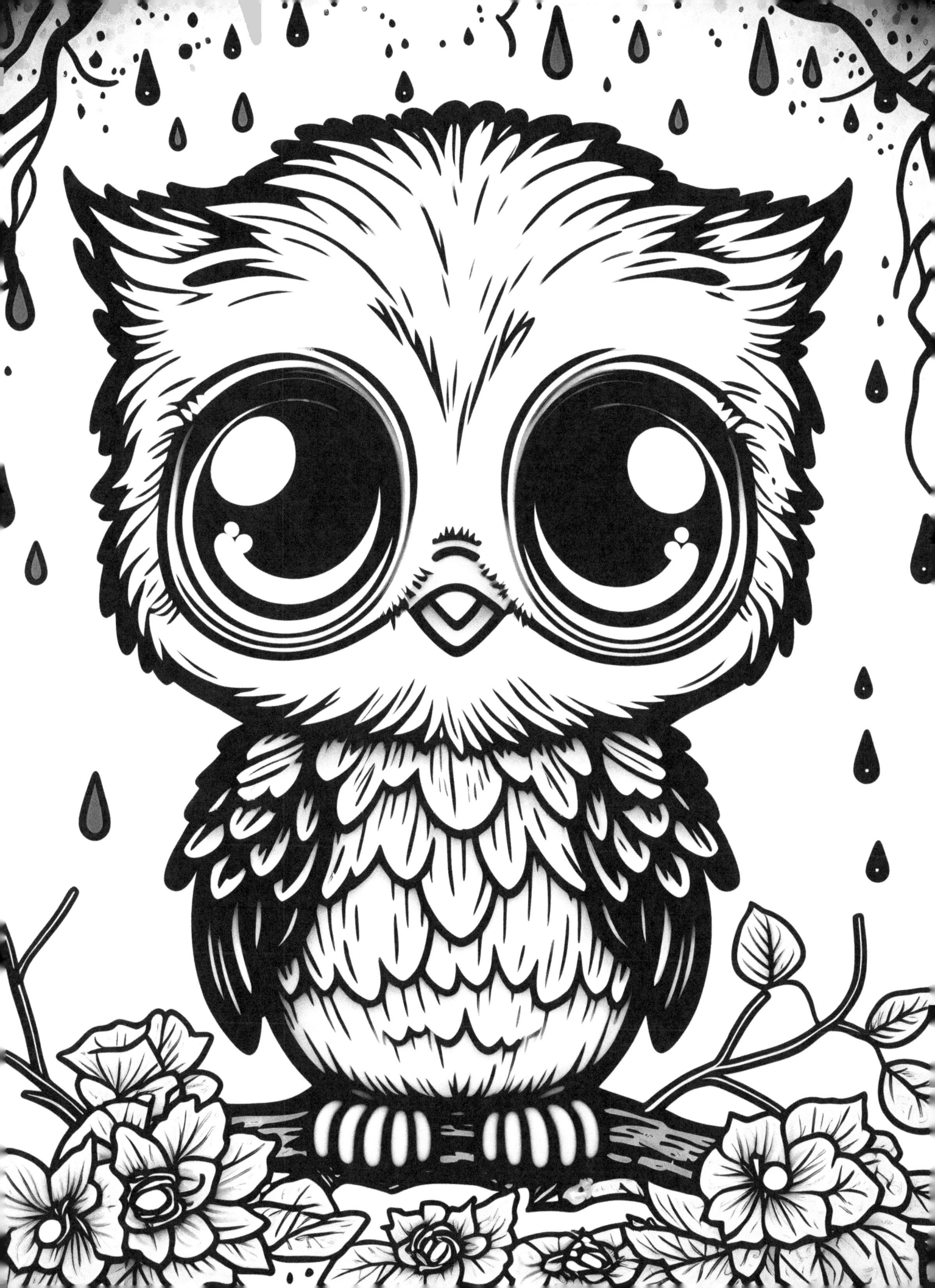

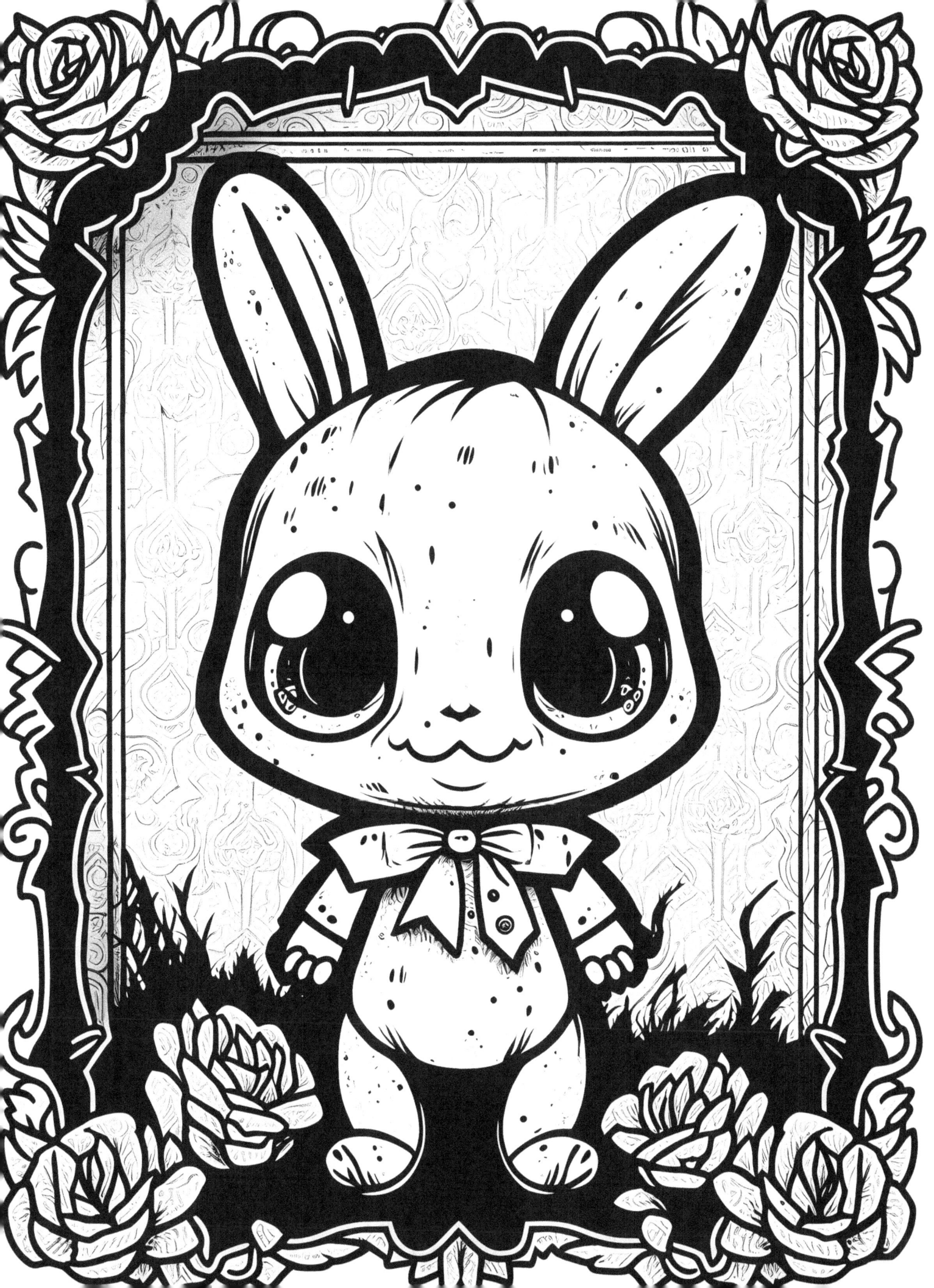

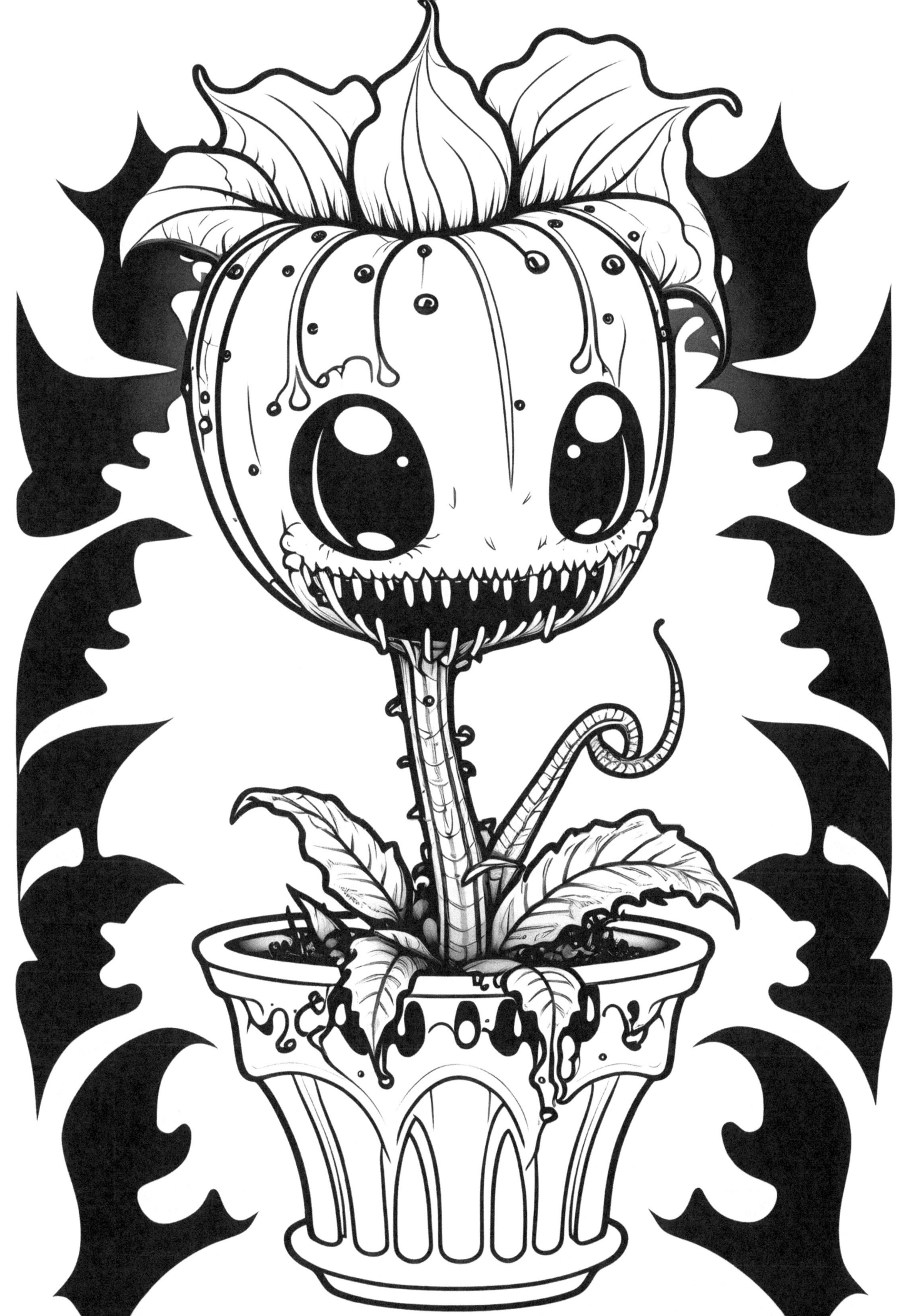

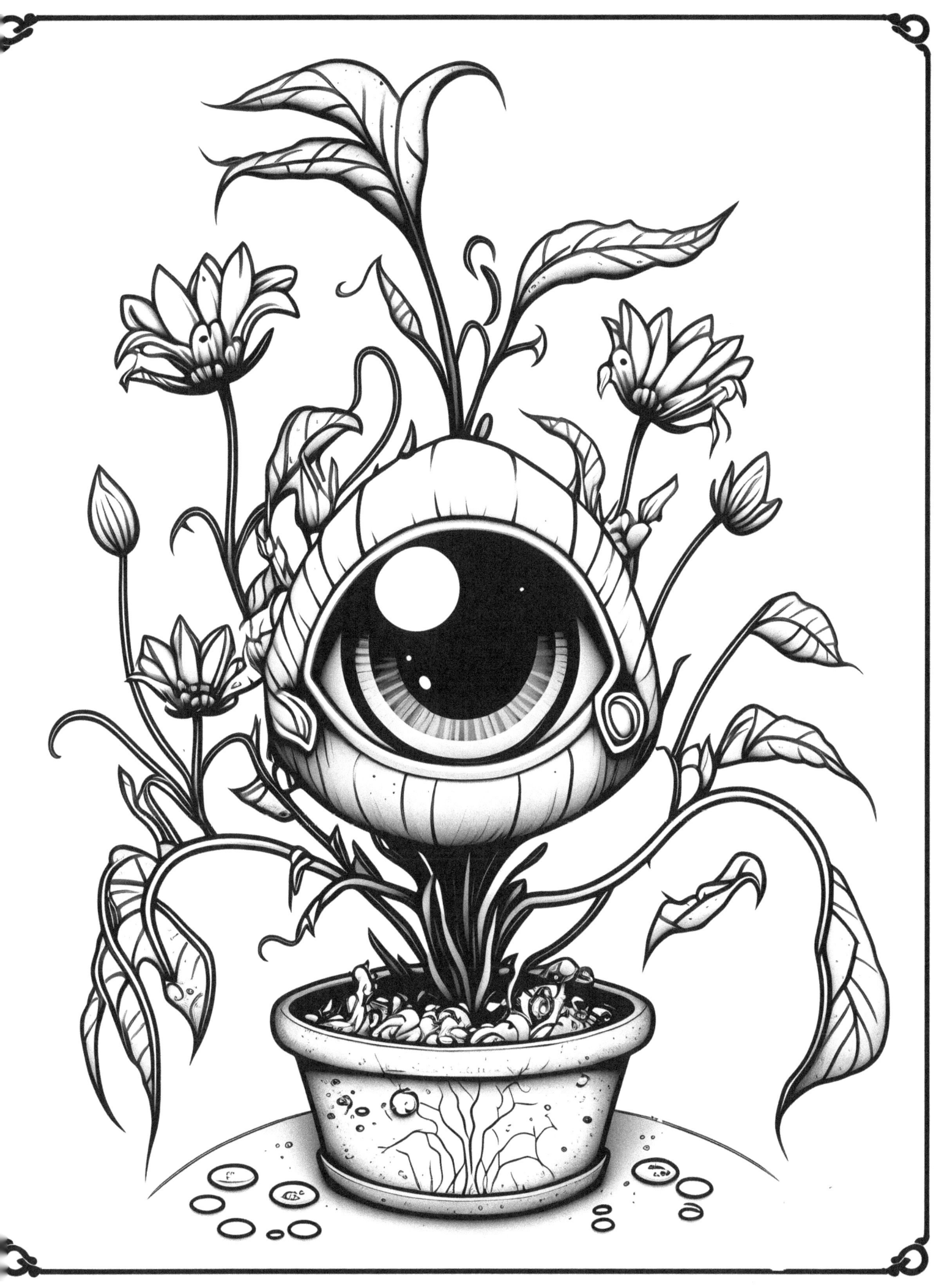

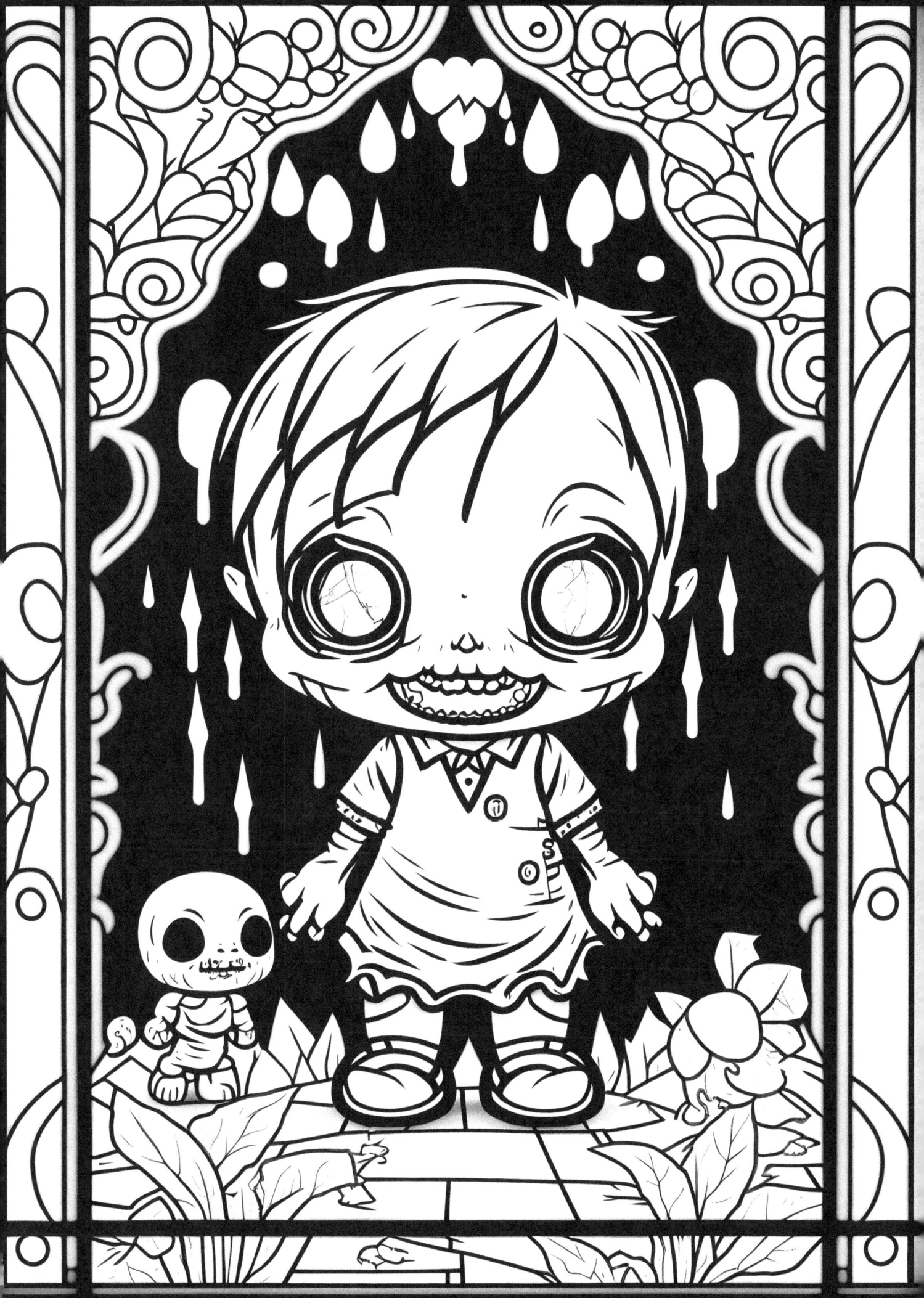

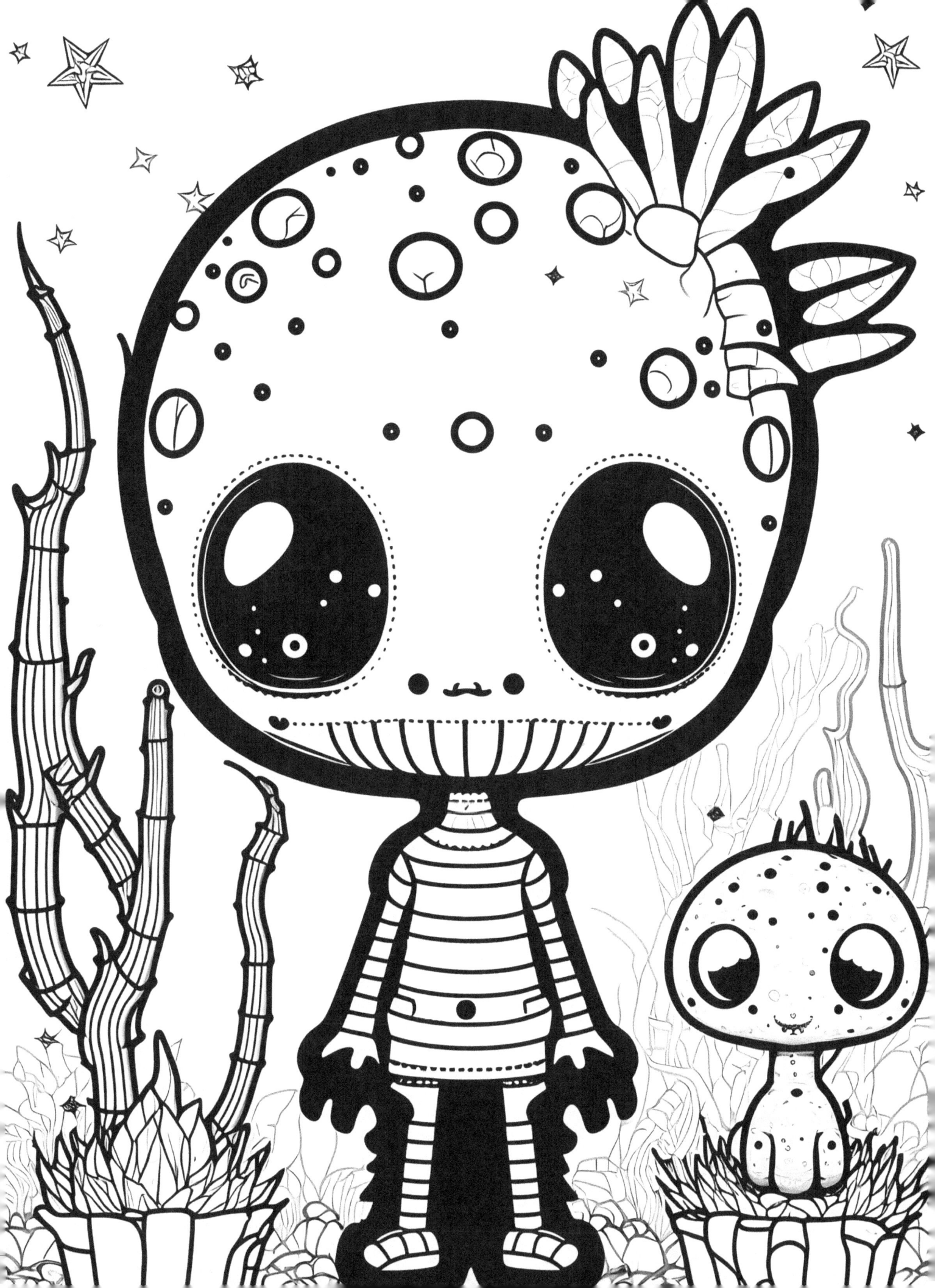

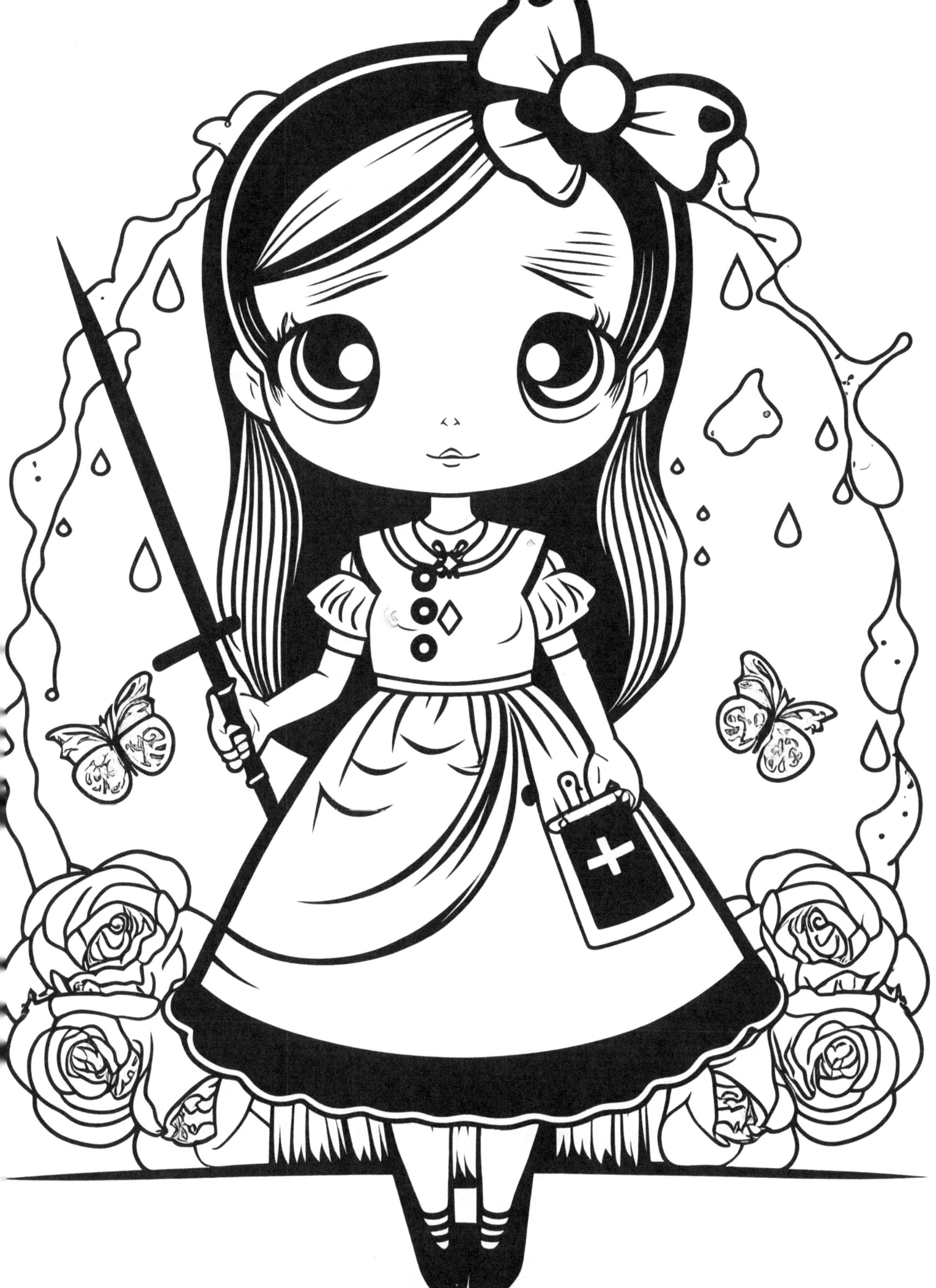

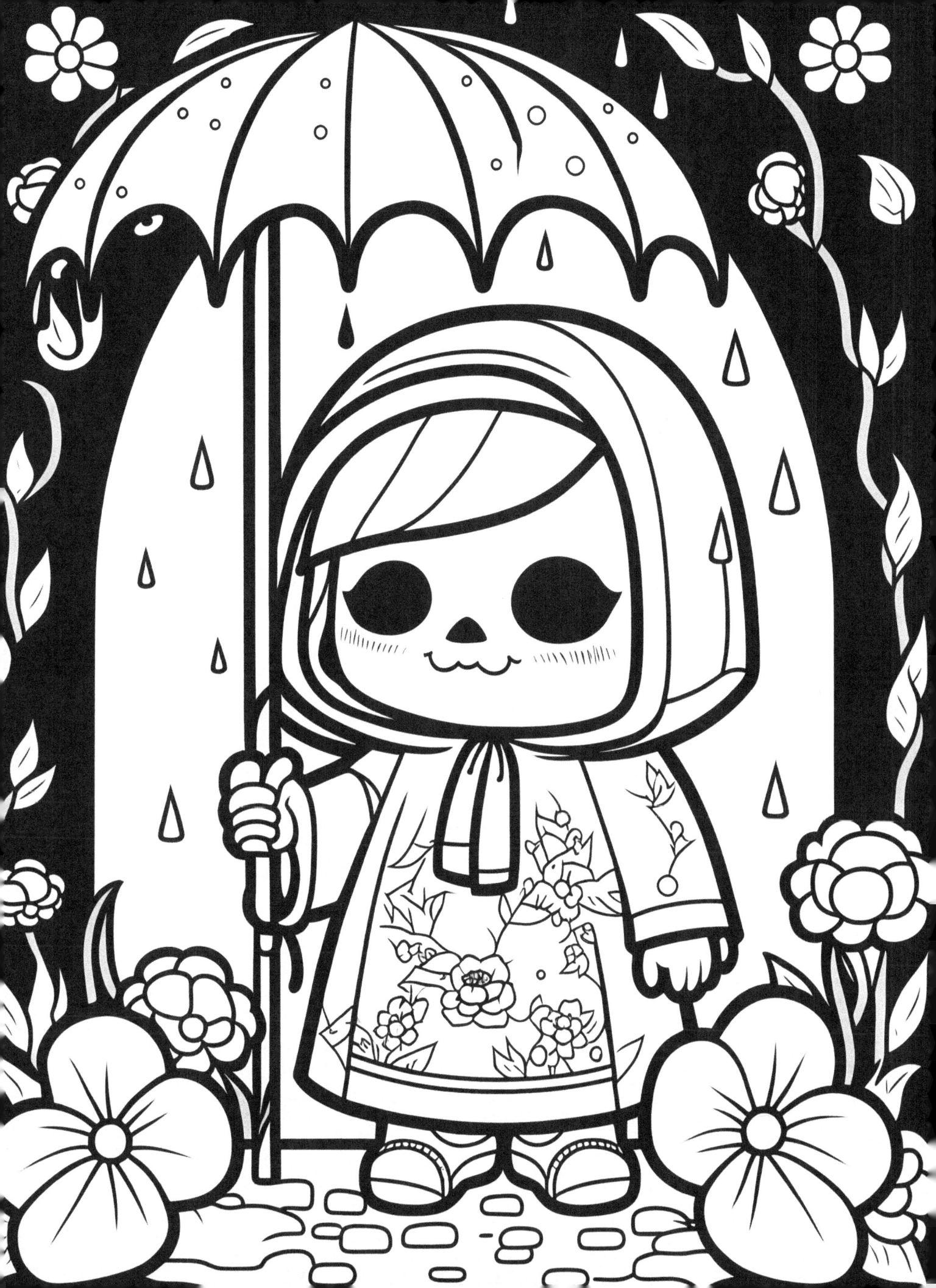

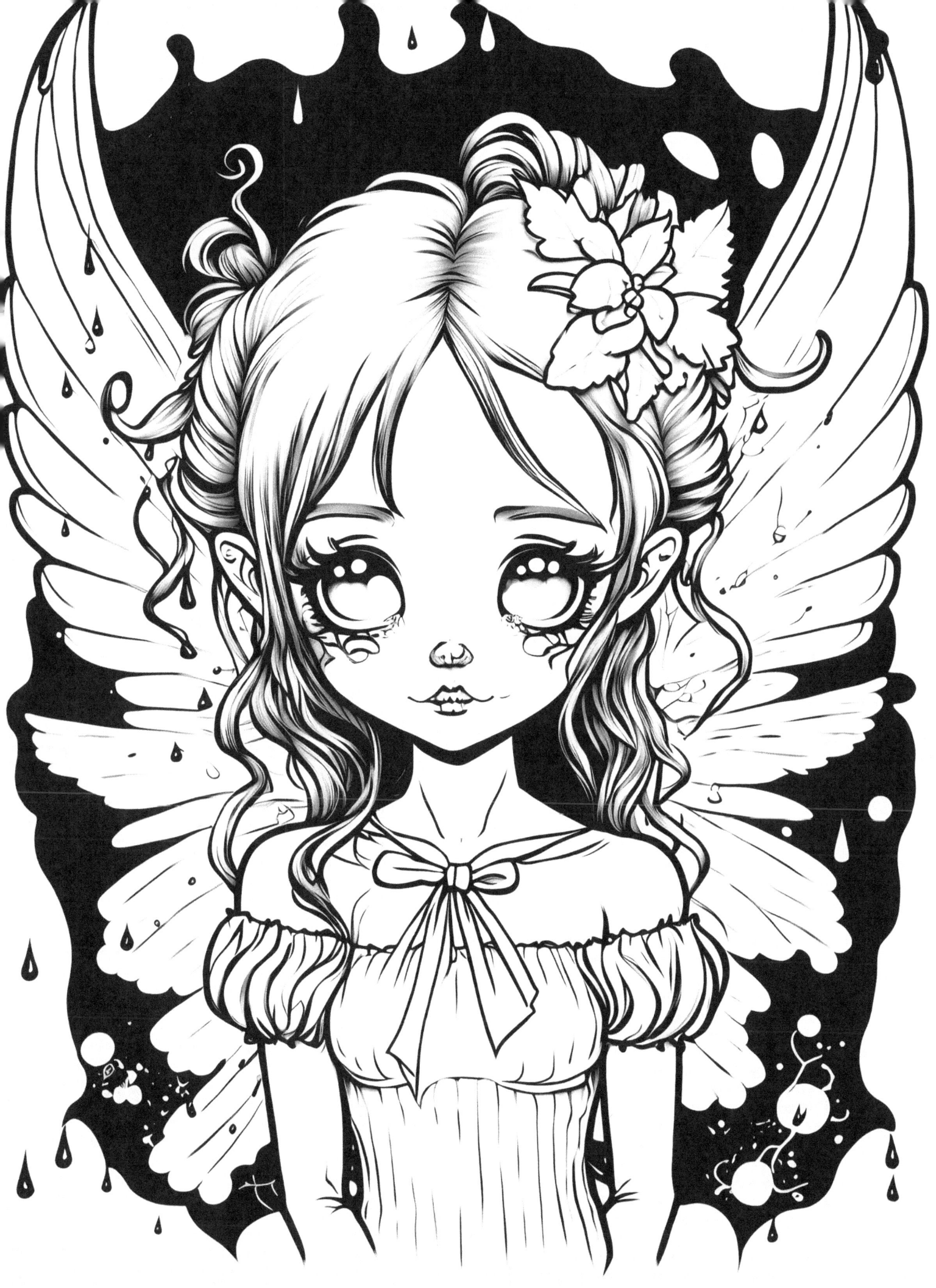

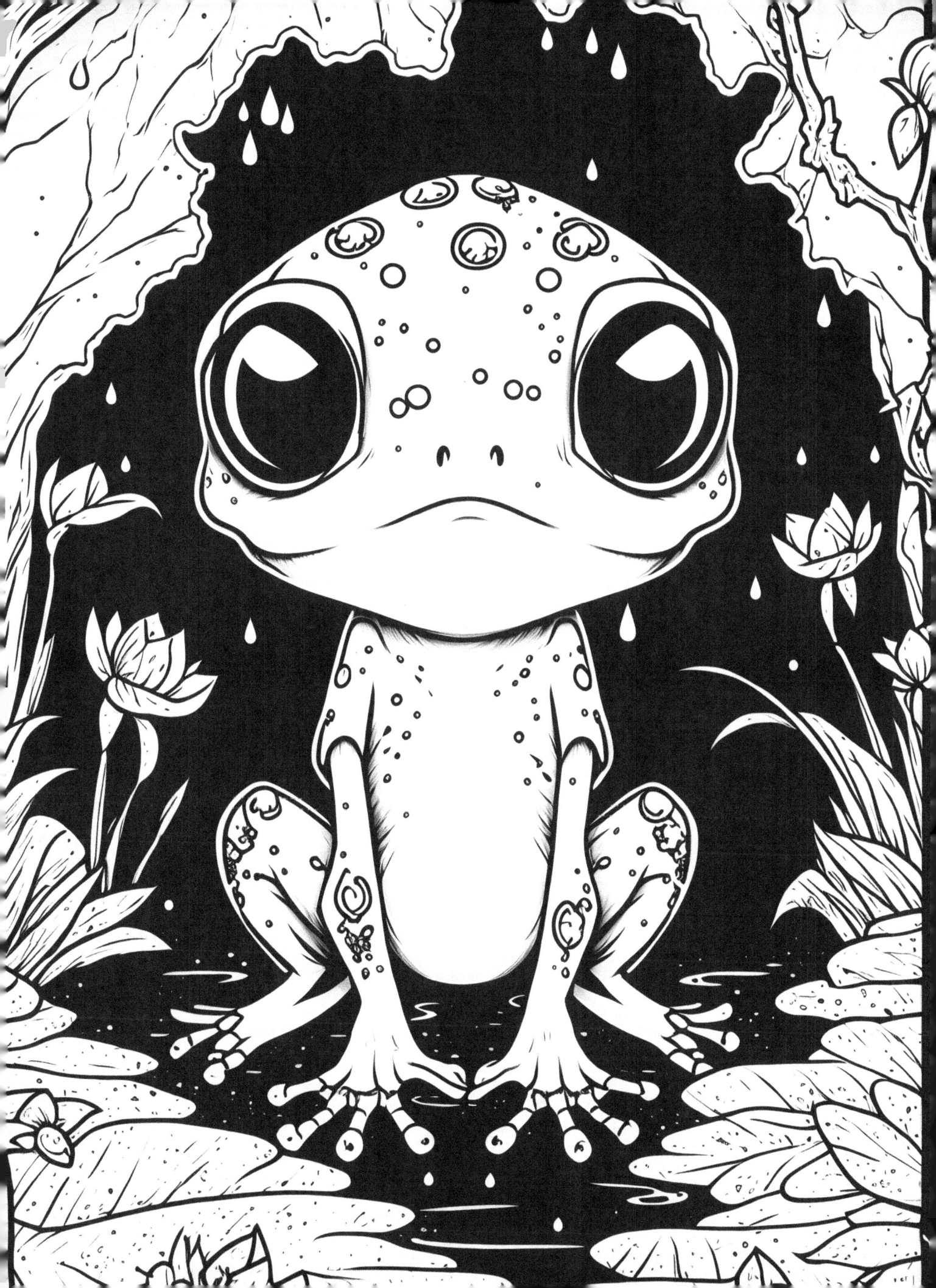

Color Test

Color Test

Color Test